Praise for
The Creative Memories Way

"One of the most valuable contributions a mom can make to her family is to serve as a memory-keeper. Many MOPS moms love the Creative Memories way! Open up this book and enter a world of help for your role as memory-keeper."

> —ELISA MORGAN
> president/CEO of MOPS International

"*The Creative Memories Way* has reminded me that album making is much more than a hobby, it is a timeless gift to my family for generations to come. Pictures are worth a thousand words, and with journaling they are worth a million. When we create memory albums, we are making a priceless investment in the people we love and, subsequently, in the future."

> —LISA WHELCHEL
> actress ("Blair" from *The Facts of Life*), author of *The Facts of Life and Other Lessons My Father Taught Me*

"Being in a family dedicated to public service, I have collected and saved many historical and personal pictures that mean so much to me. I've had the privilege to view history from the front row, and more than anything, I want to preserve these memories for my children. The task seemed too overwhelming until I was introduced to Creative Memories. I started cropping and have made several wonderful albums—and will continue making them."

> —DORO BUSH KOCH
> sister to President George W. Bush

"This is a beautiful book. It inspires us to hold on to lovely memories and treasured moments with pictures. Pictures and words in albums—with designs and unique borders. Books to open, then we smile and recall things that are important. Do not miss this!"

—ANN KIEMEL ANDERSON

author

"In our world of chaos and uncertainty, making albums reinforces and reminds us of the importance of our family and our relationships. This book inspired me to tear open my album supplies and to get started. Through the meaningful stories and examples shared, you will be longing to record *your* story for generations to come."

—MICHELE GERBRANDT

founding editor, *Memory Makers* scrapbook magazine and books

The CREATIVE MEMORIES® WAY

Creating Keepsake Albums and

Building Your Family Legacy...

CHERYL LIGHTLE | RHONDA ANDERSON

cofounders of Creative Memories®

WITH SHARI MACDONALD

WATERBROOK
PRESS

THE CREATIVE MEMORIES® WAY
PUBLISHED BY WATERBROOK PRESS
2375 Telstar Drive, Suite 160
Colorado Springs, Colorado 80920
A division of Random House, Inc.

All Scripture quotations, unless otherwise indicated, are taken from the *Holy Bible,*
New International Version®. NIV®. Copyright © 1973, 1978, 1984 by International
Bible Society. Used by permission of Zondervan Publishing House. All rights
reserved. Scripture quotations marked (KJV) are taken from the *King James Version.*

Italics in quotations reflect the authors' added emphasis.

All the stories in this book are true and have been used with permission.

ISBN 1-57856-481-6

Library of Congress Cataloging-in-Publication Data

Lightle, Cheryl.
     The Creative Memories way : creating keepsake albums and building your family
legacy / Cheryl Lightle, Rhonda Anderson, with Shari MacDonald.
          p. cm.
     ISBN 1-57856-481-6
     1. Photograph albums. 2. Photographs—Conservation and restoration. 3. Scrapbooks.
I. Anderson, Rhonda, 1957- II. MacDonald, Shari. III. Title.

TR465 .L54 2001
771'.46—dc21

                                                                    2001055935

Printed in the United States of America
2002—First Edition

10 9 8 7 6 5 4 3 2 1

To the family storyteller.

You.

CONTENTS

SPECIAL THANKS...

To Joyce Anderson, Mac Anderson, Sarah Bartos, Kathryn Baugh, Christiane M. and Marc Belisle, Sandra Bishop, Martie Byrd, Mary Chandler, Joyce Corlett, Lee and Kristi Crum, Brandi Diamond, Linda Elliott, Kathy England, Heidi Everett, Gloria Faver, Connie Fintel, Sonja Flockhart, Amy Galloway, JoEthel Griffin, Donna Haller, Carol Ann Harris, Kathleen Hart, Liz Heaney, Lori Henderson, Kelly Henry, Peg Hesse, Susan Iida-Pederson, Lois R. Johnson, Damon and Lea Kelly, Mike and Tracy Kiefer, Tanya and Tim Klein, Lisa Kurzawa, Beth Lambdin, Fran Lawler, Melanie Leach, Kimber Lybbert, Shari MacDonald, Marlys McDonald, Tracy Meyers, Janelle Mode, Jeff and Marcy Miller, Mary Natali, Mike Nistler, Annette Piper, Missy Rice, Mercedes Rinkel, Diane Rohwer-Johnson, Jan Sargent-Sukenag, Robin Scharding, Naomi Shedd, Donna Sherman, Gina Sonaglia, Gretchen Tarpley, Kristin Thomson, Mary Lou Ungar, Kresha Waldrop, Bill and Sally Wardell, Deb Yagel, and countless others, for sharing with us your stories, and therefore, your lives.

To our kids: Jacob, Joel, Janetta, and Julia Anderson,
and Brad, Shelly, and Rob Lightle,
for sharing with us your lives, and therefore, your stories.

And to our Creative Memories consultants,
for spreading the message of keepsake albums and family legacies—
and for providing the resources, the knowledge, and the
encouragement to help make them a reality.

We'd also like to thank Ada Kanning, for teaching us to embrace the tradition of creating keepsake albums; Ken Sandee, for recognizing the benefits of album making from the very beginning and for encouraging Rhonda to spread the vision; Lee Morgan, CEO of the Antioch Company, for having faith in us and supporting us as the vision of Creative Memories was realized; the staff at Creative Memories, for their unyielding devotion to our mission; Neil H. Offen of the Direct Selling Association for, from our earliest days, faithfully providing information and education to help us share our mission; Heidi Everett, for brainstorming, facilitating countless details, and seeing this book through to completion; Shari MacDonald, for believing in our vision and translating it beautifully into book form; and Liz Heaney and WaterBrook Press, for inviting and enabling us to share our story and to help you, the reader, capture *your* story.

INTRODUCTION

What is your favorite photograph of yourself as a child? Is it a picture of you with the garden hose in hand, spraying the garden—or the living room rug? Or is it the one of you sitting in a mud puddle, happily splashing away (to your mother's great chagrin)?

Or perhaps your favorite photo was taken at your wedding. Consider the shot of you and your beloved snapped by an amateur family photographer when you were completely unaware—or the professional photograph of the two of you shoving wedding cake toward each other's open, laughing mouths.

Maybe you have a treasured photo of you with your mom or dad, taken during a special fishing trip or at a church tea. Your parent may have passed away—or perhaps you have moved away—and this photograph vividly reminds you of the wonderful times you shared.

If you have photographs like these safely tucked away in an album, you are fortunate.

You are also in the minority.

Incredibly, most of us have stacks of treasured photographs that we never bother to get into albums, where they can be cherished and enjoyed. Even fewer of us take the time to document with words the powerful stories from our lives and the lives of our loved ones.

But thankfully, this situation is changing. For more than a decade, we have been helping people from all walks of life—couples and singles, women and men, parents and those without kids—get their priceless photographs into meaningful keepsake albums that they and their families can treasure. Perhaps you have a nagging sense that you want to get your photographs into albums, but you may not know where to start. Or maybe you're already an album-making enthusiast looking for additional inspiration and tips. In either case, you've come to the right place.

In this book, we will share with you our stories—and the stories of dozens of others whose lives have been forever changed by the tradition of album making. More than just sharing these heartwarming stories, though, we'll help you catch the vision for how you can experience the same blessings.

In the following pages, we will describe the many benefits of making albums, and we will show you why it is urgent for you to begin today. We will address your fears and your concerns, encourage you to develop your own vision for album making, and walk you through the basics of getting started. We'll show you how albums can help you pass on your family history to your children (if you have kids now or hope to someday) and add joy and excitement to *your* life today.

You'll read the stories of people just like you who have discovered the satisfaction and joy of making keepsake albums. You'll learn why it's important to preserve the past, and you'll come to understand the importance of documenting the lives of both children and adults. You'll discover how you can bless others through your album making efforts, and you'll see those efforts deeply enrich your life. You'll also see how you can use your albums to record life's lessons, heal life's hurts, and help you recognize signs of the miraculous in your daily experience.

Since 1987, we—Rhonda Anderson and Cheryl Lightle, cofounders of Creative Memories—have been working to bring beautiful, photosafe keepsake albums into people's homes and, more importantly, *to help people fill them with memories.* When we started working together, we had no idea that what we were about to introduce would start a new world trend. Our goal was simply to help people enrich their lives by getting their pictures and stories into photosafe albums.

Rhonda: It all started with a simple workshop I gave at a mothers' group. Since I was a little girl, I have, under my mother Ada Kanning's direction, been faithfully putting my photographs into albums. I assumed that everyone else was doing the same thing. But when my sister asked me to teach a class at a Mothers of Preschoolers (MOPS) meeting in 1987, I decided to teach a class on putting together photo albums. At the time, I was thinking, *No one will want me to teach them how to do that! Doesn't everybody do this already?* However, I had no ideas about what else I might teach, so I went ahead with my plan.

I quickly typed up a handout and proceeded to teach the class all I knew about creating photo albums. I explained why it's crucial that we make albums: It's a tradition that builds self-esteem and a sense of belonging in our children; photo albums that include journaling are fun and entertaining; and an investment in a good album is an investment in family history.

I also shared ideas about how to create albums: put names and dates beside the photos, trim each picture to focus on the important part, and use stickers to decorate the page after you have done your writing.

The response was astounding! It soon became clear that people were connecting with what I had to share. After my presentation, I was surrounded by people whose life stories were stored not in photo albums, but in shoeboxes under the bed! I couldn't believe the number of people who had done nothing with their photographs. Five of the women asked me to come to their homes to share my presentation with their friends, and forty wanted to know where they could buy albums like mine!

I started doing home presentations and ordering in bulk from Webway, the company that made the albums that my mom used and that I was still using. Everywhere I went, the reaction was the same: if eight people were there, all eight wanted to buy a photo album! I thought, *You know, there's something to this idea here. Obviously not everybody has their pictures in photo albums as I thought!*

With this in mind, I decided to consult a friend and attorney to get his opinion about the response I was having to those first album classes. As I explained to him that people were keeping their pictures in shoeboxes under the bed and that they needed both motivation to make albums and practical help to do it, he sat poring over one of my family albums. When I'd finished, he looked at me seriously and said, "Rhonda, every day people come to my office filled with despair. They are so discouraged about life; they have no hope. If only they had albums like these to look back and *remember* all the good things that have happened and all the reasons why life is worth living, I know they would have the hope to go on. *Everyone needs to have albums like these.*"

That very afternoon, I placed a call to Webway, where I reached Cheryl Lightle. Soon, we were working out a plan of action to help families get their photographs out of shoeboxes and into albums.

Together, we talked about those initial presentations, which were inspiring a demand for countless albums. From that phone call evolved our vision that one day thousands of people would be giving presentations, selling albums, and spreading the photo-preservation message.

That vision grew, and after many months of research and development, Creative Memories became a reality. Today, Creative Memories is a direct-selling company represented by tens of thousands of consultants, and our photo preservation tradition is being taught around the world, including the United States, Canada, Australia, the United Kingdom, New Zealand, Taiwan, Germany, and Japan. Everywhere you turn, people are preserving their photographs "the Creative Memories way."

Of course, much has changed since that first phone call. Since then, Creative Memories has grown beyond anything we could have imagined—and so has the scrapbooking industry. The *Wall Street Journal* has called scrapbooking the hottest trend in the craft industry.[1] Susan Brandt, spokesperson for the Hobby Industry Association, said that scrapbooking* is "absolutely the fastest moving trend we've seen in this industry."[2]

Ask those involved in the hobby [scrapbooking], and they'll tell you that its phenomenal growth is due almost exclusively to the efforts of a single company, Creative Memories, a St. Cloud, Minnesota-based supplier of scrapbooking products whose home parties continue to be the first experience most hobbyists have with the activity.[3]

But Creative Memories is more than just a photo album company. We are about *tradition,* and we have been since the very beginning. We are about legacies. Without this higher purpose, we would be just another album company.

---

* Although *scrapbooking* is the term generally applied to the work promoted by album companies, you'll see in the chapters ahead that we prefer to use the terms *album making* as much as possible. The reason is that *scrapbooking* is viewed as a hobby or a craft, while making keepsake albums is about building connections, enriching our lives, and leaving a lasting family legacy.

With it, we are, have been, and will continue to be an integral part of a move-ment to bridge generations.

We can say without a doubt that more than a dozen years ago, when Rhonda taught that first in-home class, the forty women who flocked to the front of the room didn't respond because they loved the technical aspects of her album. The major emphases of her presentation were the benefits of hav-ing an album, what the album would do for their families, and how they could make the albums themselves.

It's the same message we have for you: Someday you may regret the time you spent working or watching television, but you'll never regret the time you took to create a lasting legacy.

The memories are yours to capture, to celebrate, and to keep. We're just here to get you started—and to cheer you on along the way.

PART I

Catching the Vision

Peggy used to have a huge salad bowl on top
of the refrigerator, full of undeveloped film.
She had written on each cartridge what year
and for what event the snapshots were taken.
She and [her husband] Danny would occasionally
get the big bowl down and look at the rolls.
"Oh, Danny, look, Grand Canyon 1974,
Chris was two. I'll bet these are good."
—*Get Your Act Together: A 7-Day Get-Organized Program*
for the Overworked, Overbooked, and Overwhelmed
by Sidetracked Home Executives
Pam Young and Peggy Jones (a.k.a. The Slob Sisters)

"What is the use of a book," thought Alice,
"without pictures or conversations?"
—LEWIS CARROLL, *Alice in Wonderland*

Chapter One

EVERYBODY HAS A STORY TO TELL

Wherever men have lived
there is a story to be told.
—HENRY DAVID THOREAU, *Journal*

I myself, I am not a character
in this novel; I am the novel.
—PHILIP K. DICK, *A Scanner Darkly*

Everybody has a story to tell—including you.

You may not realize it yet (so few of us do), but your life is an incredible, compelling, page-turning story. To those who love you most—and to generations yet to be born—it is more enthralling than the most spellbinding bestseller. It is a beautiful composition that has been crafted since before you entered this world—and it is still being written.

The visual images are there (photographs that are probably stuffed in a shoe box under your bed, piled loose and curling in drawers, or packed away in your attic). So are the words. (They're the stories you tell your friends, your deepest thoughts, your secret and not-so-secret dreams.) They just haven't made it onto paper, into an accessible, easy-to-read, and enjoyable format...yet.

But they will. For you hold in your hands a book that will inspire you not only to bring your treasured photographs, memorabilia, and stories together into albums you and your family can treasure, but to do so in ways that will preserve your past, enrich your present, and inspire hope for your future.

That sounds like a lot to ask from a photo album. But we're not talking about any old album. And you aren't just any storyteller. You—and only you—hold the keys to thousands of stories and details that will make your memories come alive. You and your family can soon be enjoying the strengthened relationships, richer communication, increased self-esteem, and feelings of thankfulness and belonging that album making has brought to thousands of lives.

And it's easier to do than you might think.

Oh, you may feel overwhelmed by the mere thought of getting your photographs into albums. You're not alone. Every day we meet people who share your apprehension. But album making is, in fact, much more doable than most of us realize—and it's getting easier all the time. Best of all, as the stories in this book illustrate, it is infinitely worth the effort. We think you'll agree. Before long you, too, can be rolling up your sleeves, getting your hands on those piles of important but long-ignored photographs, and enjoying every minute of the process!

If you're like most people, you're probably thinking, *But my life isn't that interesting. In fact, it's downright average.* Or you may feel that you haven't accomplished enough yet to make your life meaningful. We couldn't disagree more strongly. In the following pages, we will show you just how truly important your life story and the story of your family are—to you, to those you love, and to generations to come.

EVERY LIFE CAN READ LIKE A BESTSELLER

In *Leaving a Trace: The Art of Transforming a Life into Stories,* author Alexandra Johnson tells of a diary she was given. It was written by a young woman named Elizabeth Howe, who in the late 1800s lived in the house that Johnson had bought one century later. Johnson beautifully describes what happened as she pored over the personal details Howe shared:

With each page, a stranger's life slowly unfolded: waiting for someone named Charlie to return from college; having her ice skates sharpened at a nearby frozen pond; going into Boston with her sister Mattie to buy sheet music; celebrating her twenty-first birthday, glad the absent young man had sent violets that survived a snowstorm.

Could she have imagined how a century later someone in her own house would be fascinated by the clues she left of a life that probably seemed immensely dull to her at the time? Was it her only diary? I needed to know: What happened late that summer of 1895? Did Charlie vanish? How did he finally break her heart? I hoped that heartbreak wasn't lurking in the unexpected: those pale gray eyes of her close friend Kitty. Toward the diary's end the handwriting is frantic— the loops of the l's swell like lungs bursting.

As I closed Elizabeth Howe's diary, I thought about how, if we can't keep diaries ourselves, we still love reading others', eavesdropping on lives in private conversation with themselves. With each page I watched Howe try to find a narrative shape for her life, a way to tell its story, if only to herself. In stolen private moments, her hand recorded what I'm sure her brain constantly told her was of no importance: her life. From her journal I knew hers was a quiet but hungrily alive life. The pages chronicled a twenty-one-year-old music teacher secretly thrilled by solitude, love letters, fresh peaches wrapped in tissue, ice storms filigreeing the windows at night with crystal spiderwebs.[1]

With every seemingly insignificant detail, Howe's diary drew Johnson further in until she, in many ways, intimately knew the woman telling the story. And the two weren't even related! It's likely that just from the text excerpted above, you now know Elizabeth Howe better than you do your own great-grandmother. What small things caused her heart to thrill? What was her handwriting like? Who was her first love?

What about you? What will your own great-grandchildren know about you one day? Will they know how you met your spouse? Your favorite flavor of ice cream? Your most embarrassing moment? Your spiritual beliefs? Will they know even more personal stories? Will they know about the person you *almost* married? About the childhood dream that came true later in life? About the impact you long to have on this world?

What are you doing today to create a legacy your descendants will cherish tomorrow?

Howe's diary not only preserves in detail the story of a life richly lived, but it also helps us recognize the vacuum that is created when life stories are forgotten. In one passage, Howe describes an afternoon's work she performed for pocket money: At a cemetery slotted for relocation, she was charged with the task of copying names from gravestones into a ledger. To the young Elizabeth's dismay, several of the gravestones were indecipherable—impossible even to "read" by tracing her fingers along the lines carved into the stone. As a result, the names were lost forever—as though the people to whom they belonged had never walked the earth. That loss deeply disturbed Howe. Yet she could do nothing to recapture any record of the lives of those buried in the cemetery. "Knowing what each [person] had accomplished within a life" after they were gone, Johnson reflects, "was as hard as guessing the color of their eyes."[2]

WILL YOUR NAME—OR WORSE—BE LOST?

What would you give to have a diary like Elizabeth Howe's written by your father's grandmother or your mother's great-great-grandfather? Sadly, few of us have any written record of our ancestors' lives. Often, all we have are stories passed down through the family tree—and only a few generations' worth at the most. As our loved ones pass away, many of these stories are being lost as well.

We think we know the stories; we've heard them—or snatches of them—in delicious (and, at times, agonizing) detail all our lives. But when we think to write them down, we find that we have several stories mixed or confused, or we are unsure about important details: "Did my grandfather trade two chickens for our old clawfoot table, or was it five?" "Why, exactly, was my mother's grandfather kicked out of Germany—and how did he escape?," or "Why was Great-grandma Inez, with her crippled hand, the one to climb up to fix the roof of the house?" Far too often, these priceless stories never get written down and precious photographs are not preserved, and therefore are ultimately lost.

You've probably heard the popular question, "What would you be sure to get out of your house if your house caught on fire?" Most of us answer something like, "My children, my pets, and my photos." Yet those same photos that we would want so badly to rescue from the flames are generally stashed, forgotten, in boxes under the bed! At some point we need to stop and ask ourselves: If the photographs are *that* important to us, why aren't we enjoying them while we have them?

For many of us, disorganization compounds the problem.

"I inherited the ability to scatter photos throughout the house," Peg Hesse told us. As a result, she says, "my pictures wound up in boxes with bills and other things. Eventually, many were cleaned out or thrown away with paperwork. In the course of moving various times, my collection of pictures also decreased even more. If I had put those photos in an album, I would have them now to enjoy.

What Is Acid-Free?

We are often asked, "Does acid-free also mean photo safe?" Actually, the two phrases are related, but different.

Not all acid-free products are photo safe. Acid free is only one aspect of being photo safe. For example, cooking oil is acid-free, but it is not considered photo safe.

Here are some terms you should know:

- *Photo-safe:* The product will not harm your photos.
- *Acid-free:* The pH level will not harm your photos.
- *Lignin-free:* The paper will maintain its durability and resist yellowing.

To protect your memories, purchase high quality, photo-safe albums. Stay away from magnetic albums and pocket page albums. Look for an album with acid-free paper and a binding that allows the pages to lie flat. (This will make both reading and writing—which you're going to do a lot of—much easier.)

"Instead, I have pictures in my mind, but I can't share the memories with anyone else. I'm thinking, in particular, of a photo I took when my parents, grandparents, son, and I went on a trip to Florida. We spent one day at Disney World. While we were there, I took a picture of my grandparents sitting on a bench. It was a wonderful picture because my grandfather was wearing Mickey Mouse ears and had this huge grin on his face. The entire family loved it. Unfortunately, I have it committed to memory only."

Of course, some photographs do make it into albums. Yet often, even these are not safely preserved. In fact, many albums actually do more harm than good. This is because the chemicals used to make them not only cause the photographs to yellow but greatly increase their rate of deterioration. Some albums with magnetic, "press and stick" pages release peroxides, causing our favorite photographs to fade and discolor—and some magnetic pages adhere themselves to the photos themselves, causing permanent damage. Other popular plastic, slip-in, pocket-style albums contain a chemical called polyvinyl chloride (PVC) that releases chlorine gas, also proven to cause the fading and discoloration of photographs. Even most construction paper scrapbooks are a danger to your photos because the high-acid content of their pages causes fading and crumbling.

We believe that every family can benefit from the tradition of preserving photos in safe, meaningful family albums.

All traditions have to start somewhere, and this one is no exception. If your family is going to enjoy the benefits of completed albums, someone has to take the first step.

If you don't do it, who will?

BUT I...

Of course, we all have reasons why we think we can't put our photos into keepsake albums. So before we go any further, we want to tackle head-on the concerns we hear most often: time, handwriting, space, and creativity.

Who Has the Time?

When people think about starting an album-making tradition, time can quickly become an issue. Can you honestly say that you have room in your life for one more thing? Do you have endless, empty hours and no idea how to fill them? Do you often find yourself thinking, *What I really need is another activity to help me fill up my days?* No? We didn't think so. Frankly, neither of us "has time" to complete our albums either.

However, we believe that this activity is important enough to *find* the time, to carve it out of schedules that are bursting at the seams. In order to do so, we have had to make some tough choices. We've had to identify our priorities and decide how we're going to spend our time.

The first page of *Work a 4-Hour Day,* written by Arthur K. Robertson and William Proctor, includes this telling statistic: "Sixty-three percent of Americans want more free time to spend as they please."[3] Part of the problem, the authors claim, is that we are working today more than ever before.

Of course, Americans still do have *some* time for fun. However, most of us believe that we have even less than is actually available. "Many people feel

---

Get It Done

If you consistently work on your albums, you *will* get them done. Here are a few hints on how you can make the time to complete your keepsake albums:

- *Commit.* Set aside fifteen minutes a day, an hour a week, or three hours a month to work on your albums. Schedule this time in your planner just as you would a dentist appointment or business meeting.
- *Do double-duty.* Crop photos while you watch television. Lay out pages during your child's music/dance/hockey lessons. Mount photos while you wait for your doctor/dentist/airline flight. Invest in a good bag that will allow you to take your supplies anywhere.
- *Journal for sweet dreams.* Document the photos in your album for a few minutes before you go to bed every night.

Follow these tips, and you'll have albums done before you know it!

dissatisfied because of a *perceived loss* of their leisure time," explain Robertson and Proctor. "The increased pace of life, the demands of two-career families, and the burgeoning choices that fragment free time…have made many people sense that they have less extra time than they really do."[4]

All of us have "wasted time" in our schedules that we can tap into to help us reach our dreams, including our goal of completed albums. One tool recommended by time management experts such as Robertson and Proctor is a time analysis. The process is quite simple. Over a period of a week, note how much time you spend on each activity in your life: from grooming and television watching to working at your job and managing your home (grocery shopping, meal planning and preparation, laundry, and so on). At the end of the week, add up each category to see where you actually spend your time. You may be surprised by what you discover. If you're like most people, you'll also feel compelled to make some changes.

You may find this tool helpful, you may choose to tap into other time management and inspiration resources, or you might simply do a casual mental review of your current activities and time commitments. No matter how you approach the problem of time, however, the reality is that you have choices you must make. We do, too. But the two of us are so convinced of the importance of album making that no matter what "goes" when our schedules get stretched beyond capacity, we always make sure that we take time to work on our albums.

Rhonda: My friend Martie Byrd once told me, "I don't know about you, but I honestly forget how old I am. I forget to turn off the oven. I forget to pay the Visa bill. I even forget where I hid the gum from myself. My mind is a sieve!"

Like Martie, I have a tendency to forget. But there are some things I want to make sure I always remember: like the times I sat on my Grandpa Jensen's lap in his favorite recliner, while he read the Danish Bible to me (I couldn't understand a word he said, but I still loved sitting there!), or the first words out of my son Joel's mouth when he was baptized at age four: "Mom, that water wanted me to swim in it!"

I don't want to remember these things only when I "have the

time." I don't want to remember them only in the future—after I've accomplished things like raising my kids and launching them into the world or helping to grow the company to a certain size. I want to— make that *need* to—remember the most important things in my life right now, right this moment.

We all need to make the time to remember the special as well as the everyday moments of our lives.

Have You Seen My Writing?

Another common protest to album making that we hear is "But my handwriting is terrible!" Many of us feel embarrassed or self-conscious about our penmanship or printing. The irony is that our loved ones aren't worried in the slightest about neatness. Sometimes messiness is half the fun! They simply love to see our words, written in sharp chicken scratches or curly loops by our very own hands.

Cheryl has said, "I still get a lump in my throat if I see my grandmother's handwriting. Someday, hopefully, somebody will get a lump in their throat when they see mine."

Don't let details like neatness and spelling stop you from making your albums a reality. You are writing for yourself and for those you love, not for your third-grade teacher. Don't focus on impressing others; focus on expressing your feelings: how you reacted to your first bicycle ride or how you felt about buying your first Christmas tree as an adult. Include the facts, of course, but go one step further. Write down *your feelings,* and those who read your album will come to know you better.

Although we recommend using one's own handwriting when journaling in an album, at times using the computer can be more efficient and still meaningful. For example, when Rhonda tells longer journal stories, she types the story on her computer because she types faster than she can write, and she can print out multiple copies. Because she makes a family album plus albums for each of her four children, she sometimes needs five copies of one story. She prints the stories on acid-free paper that matches her album pages exactly. When the printed copies are included in the books, they blend in beautifully.

Store Your Photos Safely

We often hear questions about how photos and albums should be stored. A good rule of thumb is: Your albums like to live where you live, so keep your albums and supplies at room temperature.

We recommend storage of albums at 77 degrees Fahrenheit (25 degrees Celsius) *or less* and in 20 to 50 percent relative humidity. Storing photos below 20 percent relative humidity may cause prints to curl or crack during handling. Storing photographs at high relative humidity levels can result in fungal growth. If you do not have a temperature/humidity gauge in your home, you can purchase one in an electronics or hardware store.

Keep these other important storage tips in mind:

- Do not leave your film, camera, photo albums, or supplies in your car. According to the Eastman Kodak Company, the temperature in a car with all its windows closed can reach 160 degrees in many places in the United States.
- When moving, pack your albums in an upright position. This ensures that all the weight hangs directly on the album's binding system, so photos and memorabilia do not become damaged from any excess weight on them. Do not cover the box with plastic; it can trap heat and humidity. Make sure no heavy objects are packed on top of your box of albums. Keep the box with you so you can monitor the temperature.
- Keep your albums away from ultraviolet light, excess humidity, and temperature extremes, such as you might find in the attic or basement. These factors will accelerate photo deterioration.
- At airports, keep unprocessed film in your carry-on to avoid the new baggage scanning technology, which may fog film.
- Put an index card with your name, address, and phone number in your camera case and use the first photo of every roll to take a picture of that card. Then, if your film gets separated from its envelope during processing, your photographs can find their way back to you.

Many people are hooked on the alternative of using the computer. You may be, too. But don't let it keep you from getting your handwriting in your albums as well.

But I Don't Have the Space to Make Albums!

We all know that space is a precious commodity in a home—particularly when there are small children around. It seems that every square inch can get filled up with Legos and Beanie Babies, dirty gym socks and homework projects. Sometimes it's hard to imagine ourselves clearing a spot to eat a simple dinner of macaroni and cheese, much less to spread out and work on our albums.

But, contrary to popular belief, album making doesn't require massive amounts of space. You can share album-making space with a friend, at her house or yours. You may keep your album-making materials in a portable bag and work on your pages either at local workshops set up for exactly that purpose or in your home. Or, like Rhonda, you may come up with a creative use of the space that is available to you.

> **Rhonda**: When my kids were little and I was short of space, I used to make photo album pages on the top of my portable dishwasher. It was just tall enough so the little hands couldn't reach up and grab my pens or stickers. It wasn't the most elaborate set-up in the world. But it worked. I focused on simple pages. I got my albums done.

Using the space at hand, Rhonda created a legacy that her children enjoy today and will enjoy long after she's no longer on this earth. It's a legacy that her children and her children's children will share in. Generations she will never live to see will know what she believed, what was important to her, how much she loved her family, and what lessons she learned in this life.

But I'm Not Creative!

We can't tell you how many people we've met who have balked at the prospect of starting their albums simply because they believe they're "not creative." Nonsense! We are all creative. *You* are creative. No matter how you put together your albums, they will be a reflection of the distinctive person that is

you. You can't help but create albums that are personalized. That personaliza-
tion is what makes them creative. *You* are the "creative" in Creative Memories.

Even those of us who don't consider ourselves artists find that the motivation to do something with our photos brings out an artistic side of us we
didn't even know we had.

Album maker Kathy England told us, "I am not an artistic person by
nature." But, she says, "Something in photos stirs me. And as I become older
the photos and memorabilia mean even more."

One of Kathy's favorite two-page spreads in her album is quite simple.
One side reads "Interview with Mom" spelled out in letter stickers that are
placed vertically on the page; the other side reads "Interview with Dad." Each

---

tip

Album Making:
It's Not Just for Women Anymore

Since the tradition of making keepsake albums began, women have carried much of the responsibility for making their family albums a reality.
Yet in numerous households, that pattern is changing. Men everywhere
are beginning to reclaim and share the role of family storyteller.

Inspired by the albums his wife created, Damon Kelly decided to
create albums of his own. "I am telling the story of my love for my
family," he says. "I am putting in this album pictures that are special to
me, and I am writing about how I feel about my wife and my sons." In
his own album making, Damon—like many other men—steers away
from stickers and embellishments: "My presentation is very simple and
straightforward."

Damon says to men, "Don't be afraid to tell your story. Don't
let your wife be the only one to share her heart with your children
through these albums. Your children, your wife, need to know of your
heart for them." He issues this challenge: "Step up to the plate. Cut
against the example our culture holds up for men to be like, and bless
your family with your words you have put in an album."

page includes a photograph of that parent, taken about 1950. On one page, Kathy includes her mother's story of how she met Kathy's dad; her father's page offers his version. "It's funny," she says, "they don't match up exactly. But that makes it more special." Between the two pages is a photograph of her parents together as a young couple.

Kathy has also come up with other unique ideas. Several years ago, she found a black-and-white picture of herself as a three-year-old, sitting on a tricycle. She later discovered a photograph of her husband on a tricycle, taken around the same time, which shows him facing in the same general direction. Kathy then got the idea to take a photograph of her son at three years old in a similar pose, also using black-and-white film. She plans to do the same soon with her daughter, who is now two and a half.

"You know, I used to feel that I couldn't make albums, because I didn't think I was creative enough. And I'm not artistic, that's true. I *cannot* draw a picture of a horse; it looks like a Volkswagen! But I found out that I wasn't giving myself enough credit…that I am more creative than I think."

Kathy offers this advice to those just starting out: "You *can* do it. Thirty years from now, your family may notice the stickers and the artwork and the nice touches you put on. But what they're *really* going to look at is the pictures and the journaling you put with them."

Despite the fact that she didn't see herself as traditionally artistic, Kathy found a way to access and express the creativity within her.

It helps to keep your focus on completing pages, rather than on being crafty. In our personal albums, we have always kept our pages relatively simple, and we've constantly encouraged others to do the same. In fact, our slogan at Creative Memories is "Simple Pages, Completed Albums." This is "the Creative Memories way." People often ask us why this principle is so important to us. We explain that it's a matter of form following function.

When you're creating an album, the question is, "What are you hoping to accomplish?" Are you attempting to create a work of art? Or do you want to create finished albums that will be a legacy for future generations? If your greater desire is for a legacy, then the Creative Memories way—simple pages, completed albums—is the quickest, most efficient, and least stressful way to reach your goal.

The bottom line is, we are committed to helping people like you get their pictures into albums. This requires keeping a balance between the craft/decorative focus of creating pages and the commitment to completing albums. Both aspects are important. But we believe people are more interested in completing their photo albums than in focusing their time and effort on the decorative side of creating albums. There are just too many photos waiting to be put into albums for us to become obsessed with the "artistic" angle.

In other words, don't become so focused on the "creative" that the "memories" suffer.

KEEPING YOUR EYES ON THE PRIZE

That's not to say that you *can't* be artistic with your albums or that you absolutely should not spend extra time on your pages if that's your preference. A number of people *love* to create artistic, complex pages. Statistics show that

Protect Your Most Valuable Possessions

Lori Henderson reports: "One day, when my sister Vicki was visiting my mother, they took a walk around the old Burbank neighborhood. As they walked, Vicki remarked, 'Oh, this brings back memories!' My mother, who was suffering from Alzheimer's disease, responded, 'Tell me about memories. I don't have them anymore.' "

What are your favorite or most important memories? Make a list of ten you want to get down on paper and save for posterity. Write out the first story tonight—even if it's an abbreviated version. How does it feel to revisit this old memory? How would you feel if such memories were lost?

Finally, if you were to get amnesia, which handful of memories would you most want to save? Rest easier tonight, knowing that soon, these stories will be safely captured for you and your loved ones to remember and enjoy throughout your lives.

ninety percent of all Americans actively take pictures and, according to a survey by Eastern Montana College in Billings, Montana, 76 percent of people feel that their photos are valuable enough to be preserved in albums. Our research leads us to estimate that fewer than 10 percent make albums with a heavy emphasis on craft aspects. (Although, most in this group began by making their albums simple and developed their own creative style independently.)

It has been our experience, however, that people who focus on the craft side burn out and quit more often than those who focus simply on completing their albums. Not surprisingly, those who possess finished albums they can share and enjoy are much more likely to become photo historians for life.

That is why we advocate simple pages. We want to keep our eye on the goal: completed albums. And we want you to do the same. Scrapbooking as a craft may be a retail store trend, but the tradition of making heirloom photo albums can span generations. As we said at the beginning of this chapter, *everybody has a story to tell.* Let's get those photos and words in an album!

That, of course, is what the Creative Memories way is all about.

Chapter Two

MAKING A DIFFERENCE,
PAGE BY PAGE

Every hair makes its shadow on the ground.
—SPANISH PROVERB

There is much good sleep in an old story.
—GERMAN PROVERB

After moving from California to Idaho, Janelle Mode returned to her family home for a spring visit. While she was there, her mother requested that Janelle take back the family photo albums, sort through the pictures, keep those that were of her, send her sister the pictures with her in them, and return the rest to her mother when she was done.

Janelle figured the plan had one major flaw. "I knew neither of them would probably ever get the photos into albums!"

So, with her sister's birthday and parents' anniversary quickly approaching, Janelle decided to put together albums as gifts. Though she'd felt confident all along that it was a worthy idea, the depth of emotion triggered by the project surprised her. As she worked, she says, "the memories that came flooding back were overwhelming."

Janelle admits that she has struggled somewhat over the years with self-esteem. And, as many of us have experienced, she found that she sometimes felt more in touch with negative memories related to her family of origin than with positive ones.

"I had forgotten so much of the good stuff," she says. "But the stories that would come to mind with just a glance at a picture were incredible. My dad has never told me in my adult life that he loves me. But within just three pages in the album, I have five different pictures of him holding me, taken at different events. Those pictures really helped me remember the good times.

"When my mom and dad called in amazement at the albums I'd made, I began to weep and thank them for the wonderful life they had provided for me. This whole experience was a real eyeopener for me. It showed me firsthand the power of a picture and why we need to capture those moments before they are lost."

HOW DO WE LOVE OUR ALBUMS? LET US COUNT THE WAYS...

Make no mistake about it: When people see their pictures and stories in albums, they make connections with others and lives are changed. From the mom who makes special albums for her children so that they know how loved and special they are to the sibling who helps her cancer-stricken sister leave an album legacy for her family, these real people and everyday events clearly demonstrate that, through album making, we can record our love for our family in a permanent, meaningful way. We can capture meaningful family stories that would otherwise be lost. We can create a lasting legacy that will touch our loved ones' lives and, as a result, have a real impact on the world.

Let's briefly touch upon the benefits your album-making efforts will bring.

You'll Protect Your Investment

Do you have a camera—of any kind? Digital? 35mm? Point-and-shoot? Disposable? If so, you've made an investment. Cameras, film, developing—none of these things come cheap. So why wouldn't you want to protect your investment? If you bought a bread maker and you never made bread, what would be the point? Likewise, if you take pictures that you never look at—or if you look at the pictures, but never write down the stories behind them for future generations—you are simply throwing money down the tubes.

Years ago, a woman in one of Rhonda's classes was working on her twenty-year-old prom pictures. "If only I could remember my date's name," she mourned.

It was the prom! At the time, you think, *I could never forget that it was Tony Jones who took me to the prom!* But you do forget. We all do.

By writing down your stories and pairing them with your pictures, you're carrying the popular photo-taking process through to completion and making the best possible use of your photographs and equipment.

You'll Get a Unique Opportunity to Say What's on Your Heart

We all have so much we could say to and about our loved ones: "Joel, you are an incredible leader! You can motivate a roomful of people to do anything!" "Janetta, you are such a spunky, strong spitfire!" "Shelly, you have such a compassionate heart. You'd take in every stray dog in the world if you could! You have such a kind soul." But all too often we have no reason to write them down, and these words—words that can make a powerful impression on the lives of those we care about most—go unsaid.

When we are purposeful about recording our feelings in our albums, however, many of these previously unexpressed feelings and words of encouragement make it onto the page, where they can be read by and have an impact on those we love.

At Creative Memories, we are constantly looking for new ways to get our stories and thoughts into our albums. Several months ago, our marketing department asked Cheryl to write something they called a Bio Poem. The first two lines of a Bio Poem call for the writer to give a person's name and tell who that person is. The next lines are about how that person fits into the family, what that person's hobbies are, and so on. Cheryl decided to write her Bio Poem about her daughter. At first, the process felt awkward. Then, all of a sudden, the words started flowing. Even after years of serving as Creative Memories' president, she couldn't believe what she was able to express in only a few lines:

Shelly Ann

Bright, beautiful, full of life, tenderhearted, great mom,
    always bounces back.
Sister of Brad and Rob, daughter of Ron and Cheryl,
    mother of Nick and Bailey.
Loves children and wants a houseful, loves to listen to
    Grandma Betty tell stories from the past.
Who likes to clean her own fish and take the hook out,
    fixes own car, changing radiators and brakes.
Who feels everyone else's pain, feels compelled to give
    and give, reluctant to express own feelings, hides
    behind laughs and shocking statements.
Who would take in every stray animal in her town.
Who feels strongly about giving a helping hand, and
    about missing her mom to talk to.
Who is a whiz at math and can do anything she sets her
    mind to.

Cheryl: I would never have told my daughter all those things I wrote
in the poem. I might have casually mentioned, "You know, Shelly, you
always got good math grades" or "You sure are great with kids." But
putting it all together, acknowledging who she is, made all the difference—to her and to me.

For me, the process brought a real sense of accomplishment. I'm
not a natural writer, but I do have a lot to say. I felt proud to be able to
share my feelings so completely with my daughter.

Shelly was touched—much more so than I would have expected.
In fact, when I told her I'd written even more in my rough draft, before
I chose which lines to use, she asked, "Well, can I have what else you
wrote? Can I have the original?"

Our words mean more to our loved ones than we would ever dream.
When we write about those we love in our albums, we're speaking not just to

them. It is as if we're proclaiming to the entire world how we feel. We are conveying messages that we might not have had any other opportunity to communicate or perhaps would not have felt comfortable saying face-to-face.

Best of all, what we say is lasting. Spoken words bring us moments of joy; written words bring joy that we can linger over or return to and, in both cases, savor.

It is impossible to overstate the importance of expressing ourselves to our loved ones. Often, we expect others to know how we feel by our actions rather than our words. We make our spouse's favorite dinner but forget to say, "I love

> ## (tip)
>
> ### Say "I Love You" in a Bio Poem
>
> Share your thoughts and feelings about someone close to you with a Bio Poem. A Bio Poem gives shape to the words you choose to share your feelings and thoughts.
>
> *Line 1:* Your subject's first name
> *Line 2:* Who is… (Use words that describe this person)
> *Line 3:* Who is brother or sister or child or parent of…
> *Line 4:* Who loves… (Name three ideas or people)
> *Line 5:* Who feels… (List three emotions or passions)
> *Line 6:* Who gives… (List three actions; for example, who gives great foot rubs, who selflessly gives her time to help the community, who gives from the heart)
> *Line 7:* Who fears… (List three things; for example, who fears spiders, flying, saying something that hurts someone's feelings)
> *Line 8:* Who would like to see… (List three things; for example, who would like to see peace in the world, her son's graduation, the Eiffel Tower)
> *Line 9:* Who shares… (List three things)
> *Line 10:* Who is a/an… (List three nouns)
> *Line 11:* Who is the resident of… (Write the city and state)
> *Line 12:* His or her last name

you." We call someone to apologize, but let the phone call itself serve as the apology instead of actually saying the words "I'm sorry."

Yet just three or four words can instill trust, heal wounds, cement relationships, and brighten the day in a world that can often use brightening.

That fact reminds us of a story our friend Susan Iida-Pederson told us. "One day," Susan said, "my husband and I were at a social gathering with some friends and their families. We were all seated for dinner when our friend Judy walked in. She sat at our table, and I said, 'Judy, I love your hair! It looks so great.' But others were greeting her, and there was a lot of talking. So she didn't hear me, and I let it go. Shortly after, the noise stopped, and there was one of those quiet moments in the room. That's when six-year-old Maggie tugged at my sleeve and said, 'Tell her now.' "

We love that: *Tell her now.* Such big wisdom from such a little girl! When we work on our albums, when we add stories about those we love, we have the opportunity to *tell them now.* Each week the introduction to the *Satellite Sisters* radio program, broadcast on National Public Radio, promises: "Not every conversation will change your life; but any conversation can."[1]

The same principle applies to album making. Perhaps not every word you write will speak to a loved one's heart. But your words will almost certainly have a much greater impact than you could ever imagine.

We've all heard the old saying "A picture is worth a thousand words." But we believe that a picture *without* words loses the greater part of its value. Pictures are much more powerful, lasting, and memorable when paired with the stories that go with them.

One woman told us the following story about her teenage son. We all know that teenagers have their insecurities and doubts, and this young man had had his share.

One night, his mother came downstairs and found him on the sofa looking at his photo album. As she walked in, he looked up at her and said, "You do love me, don't you?" It wasn't just the pictures that told him so. He was reading what she had written under the pictures. His mother's words, more than anything else, helped him know that he was loved. And those words were there for him to read because she had seized the opportunity to *write them down.*

You'll Connect with Your Roots

Photographs reveal to us important clues about the past. If you open up an album and see photographs from your childhood showing you doing farm chores at 6 A.M., you may say, "Gee that's why I have the work ethic I do." Or you may see pictures of yourself scrubbing down the dairy barn and think, *No wonder I'm so fastidious about washing my hands.*

Nearly a century ago, Gerard Manley Hopkins wrote, "What I do is me: for that I came."[2] Seeing our photographs in albums helps us make a connection between who we are, what we do, and why we are the way we are. Seeing our family values being lived out gives us a sense of continuity and tradition.

Cheryl, for example, has always had an outrageous sense of style. Here's an example, just to show you *how* outrageous. One day, some of the folks at Creative Memories had a "Cheryl Lightle Dress-Up Day," and one woman came wearing Christmas tree ornaments as earrings!

> **Cheryl:** I have always loved dressing flamboyantly, but I had never really thought much about where that tendency came from. Not long ago, however, I was working on my albums, and I came across a picture of myself that was taken when I was about eight years old. In the black and white photo, I was standing with my younger brothers, who were probably five and three at the time. All three of us were dressed in cute little outfits—what I call "glitzy." There were little studs on the pants, and I was wearing a jacket with a cowboy on it, flinging a lasso.
>
> I was looking at the photo, simply enjoying it, when suddenly I realized, *That's where I get it!* I have always worn big, dangly earrings and showy metal belts. I realized the tradition of flashy dressing began with the way my mother clothed me. As I look at myself and my siblings in those crazy get-ups, I feel a great sense of understanding and connection: *This is where I came from* and *So that's why I do what I do!*

Of course, photos tell only part of the story. We've heard countless tales about people—spouses, children, parents—who've received an album that was prepared for them or about them. Almost universally—like the troubled teenager we mentioned a moment ago, whose mother's words helped heal his heart—the first thing people ask about or look for is, *What did you write?*

Though many of us wish it were otherwise, the ancient art of letter writing is largely lost to us today. Writing in your albums is one of the few remaining opportunities you have to express to your children your beliefs, your desires, your feelings, your concerns, and what your life has been like so that they can understand where you came from—and therefore where *they* came from.

You'll Make People Feel Loved

Do you ever get tired of hearing that you are loved? No one does! And albums can provide numerous ways for you to express your love for others.

> **Cheryl:** A girlfriend of mine told me about a gift her parents received from their granddaughter. These people live in a beautiful home. They have everything they could want. They are the sort of individuals who make you think, *What do I buy these people?*
>
> One Christmas, their granddaughter Beth put together a tribute album for them. Later, my friend asked her mother, "What was the best present you got this year?" The answer? "That album Beth gave me. *It's the best gift I have ever received!*"

This woman could afford to purchase anything she wanted. Certainly, she had received expensive gifts before. But nothing could compare in worth to the gift that her granddaughter had lovingly created for her. The photographs from the early years of her marriage brought back romantic memories and helped her and her husband remember the many reasons they got married in the first place. Their granddaughter's journaling also showed them how she perceived them—and how much they had contributed to her life.

Our albums make people feel validated—while they're still living—and allow them to understand that they are deeply cherished and loved.

You'll Enjoy Family Fun

Not only does album making yield incredible results, but it's also a great activity for families to participate in together. In particular, we are big advocates of what we call "family crops." ("Cropping" is the practice of trimming your photos, sometimes into circles or shapes, so that the focus is on the most important part of the picture.) At these "crops," a family will sit down together to work on an album or separate albums, much the same way families used to gather to listen to the radio, play games, or work puzzles.

Not long ago, we heard from a young woman with three children, who was in the middle of a divorce. During one weekend in particular, she was feeling quite lonely. So, she started working on her scrapbook. After a while, her young children came in and started to work with her. Soon, the three of them were having a ball together! Later, she said, "It was one of the greatest evenings we've ever had." Before long, she forgot all about being lonely. Sharing her album making with her kids helped get her through.

You'll Count Your Blessings

As children in Sunday school, many of us sang the song "Count Your Blessings." In 1954's *White Christmas,* Bing Crosby urged us to do the same in the song "Count Your Blessings Instead of Sheep." What great advice—but how easy to forget! Perhaps, like us, you've experienced how tempting it is to become caught up in a frenzy of activity and effort, in the attempt to do more, acquire more, *be* more.

Yet when we take the time to slow down and review the documentation of our lives found in our albums, we often suddenly recognize that we are far more blessed than we felt. Remembering the positive keeps us going in the present and gives us hope for the future.

> **Rhonda**: Some days, I just get in a reminiscing mood. I will go to my shelf and pull out a photo album. My mom was wonderful about writing in our childhood albums. I'll read what she wrote and start pondering each page, thinking about the circumstances of when those photos were taken. It is very therapeutic to laugh at my old hairdos and to revisit so many good times.
>
> In 1961, when I was three and a half, our family went to Glacier National Park. There are several pictures of my brother, sister, and me feeding potato chips to the chipmunks. Next to those pictures of us

Mom had written: "We loved feeding potato chips to the chipmunks, except we called them 'kitties.' " You may not think that story is particularly impressive, but my kids love hearing that their mom called chipmunks "kitties"!

I'll slowly work my way through my school years and college, and then I'll arrive at the photos of my trip to Indonesia. I spent three months in a remote village on the island of Java when I was nineteen years old. My hair (back to the hairdos!) was about an inch long all over. I was sunburned so badly the first week that my eyes swelled shut. (A beautiful sight.) Then, there was the mosquito netting to sleep under, the giant cockroaches, malaria pills, and lots of poverty. The culture was very different than anything I had ever experienced. But that trip was the best thing that ever happened to me because I matured a lot during that time. Before that, I had no idea how the rest of the world really lived. It was shocking for me to realize how many blessings we have in America.

Subsequent pages show my marriage, the births of our two sons, and the arrival of our two daughters from India. My photo albums and the memories they hold always make me thank God for all he has given me.

It's so easy to become frustrated and dissatisfied with life—it happens to the best of us. At such times, our albums can ground us and put us back in touch with feelings of peace, trust, satisfaction, and contentment.

Rhonda: In the early summer of 2000, I was enjoying a brief moment at the piano, playing "Give Thanks," one of my favorite songs. The first line of the song tells us to be grateful and to give thanks. My thoughts stopped at the word "grateful," and I began to think about what having a grateful heart really meant. After looking in several places for information about gratitude, I found the following definition: "Gratefulness is honing alertness to the benefits that we possess without waiting until they are gone to appreciate them."[3]

That definition got my attention. I decided right then to become more alert to the benefits I possess while I still have them. That opportunity came sooner than I expected. Up to that point, I had been doing a substantial amount of air travel, and in July, I began experiencing sinus and ear pain. The pressure changes in the heavy humidity and air conditioning of airplanes had caused me to develop chronic sinus and ear block.

A specialist informed me that, in order to heal, I would need to make changes to my environment that included no airline travel for at least four months and minimum exposure to air conditioning.

I chose to be thankful that the diagnosis came *before* permanent damage was done: I am thankful for my hearing! I am also grateful for the time I can spend on various projects that I have wanted to develop in the past but for which I just hadn't had the time. I am grateful to be involved with a company that responded with compassion and flexibility, allowing me to work primarily from home. I am grateful that the changes in my traveling ability led my husband and me to buy a motor home—and that my family can now join me as I travel around the country for my speaking engagements.

All of this I have documented in my albums with photos and journal entries.

As you document the special events, the everyday moments, and the cherished blessings in your life, think about how much you have to be grateful for. Then, the next time you find yourself struggling to count your blessings, sit down and read over the story of your life. Savor the glittering moments that have brought you—and can continue to bring you—a heart that brims with joy.

You'll Gain a New Appreciation for Yourself

When we're asked why making albums is important, we often talk about how self-esteem grows in children when they see themselves in photo albums. (This book includes two whole chapters dedicated to the subject of children and albums.) But this principle applies not only to kids. When you go back and look at your albums, you can see what a good parent, or good spouse, or good writer or speaker (or anything else) you are. (Cheryl often looks at all those birthday cakes she decorated, all those trips to the zoo, the cookies she baked for the kids' homeroom party, and realizes, *Yeah, I was a good mom.*)

Our albums not only affirm our kids; they affirm us.

Clearly, you are never too young or too old to experience the benefits of a keepsake photo album. Whether you're two or seventy-two, you never tire of looking at pictures and hearing stories about yourself. And with good reason. After all, you are a work of art.

You'll Gain an Ultimate Argument Solver

When you have completed albums on hand, you'll have a reliable source—at last!—to turn to for family history.

> **Rhonda**: When I was growing up, my mom and dad would have the funniest disagreements! Mom would say we went to such-and-such a place in 1963. Dad would disagree. "Huh uh, that was in '64." So Mom would bet him a new mixer or set of dishes that she was correct. Then they'd go to the photo albums, and there would be the names and dates. "See!" Mom would say. "I'm right!" That's one of my most vivid childhood memories!
>
> Today, I'm seeing that same scenario replayed in my own family when we need to solve a mystery. Our albums are the supreme solvers of disagreements when it comes to questions like *When did that happen?* and *Who was there?*
>
> For example, it's a family tradition to go to Seeley Lake during the summer. One day, my daughter Julia was saying that she wasn't there one particular year. Her sister Janetta said, "Yes, you were!"
>
> In the interest of diplomacy, I won't say which daughter was right in this case! But out came the photo albums—and there was our answer in black-and-white (journaling) and full-color (photographs).
>
> Our albums frequently solve arguments in our family, and you may find that they'll do the same for you.
>
> Of course, solving arguments isn't the best or only reason to have photo albums. However, using our albums in this way does provide even more opportunities for us to get our albums out and

tip

Top Fifty Album Ideas

Here are some popular album ideas to get your creative juices flowing:

1. Heritage album
2. Family album
3. Celebration album
4. Tribute album
5. Baby album (include all the special things you notice about your new child: her scent, his soft skin, her little toes)
6. Christmas/holiday album
7. Personal album (for your child, spouse, family member, or friend)
8. ABC album (each page includes a word or headline using a letter of the alphabet, such as an alphabetical listing of your child's strengths) or 123 album (each page includes a number, such as a numerical listing of blessings; for example, 1 happy dog, 2 loving parents, 3 great kids, and so on)
9. Character album (focuses on and teaches character traits)
10. Gratitude/Thanksgiving album
11. Anniversary album (golden, silver, or other)
12. Pet album
13. Card collection album (birthday cards, holiday cards, etc.)
14. Career/professional album
15. Dream album
16. Wedding/"Our Romance" album
17. Best friends album
18. Sports/team album (either your favorite professional team or your child's sports season)
19. Coaching album (chronicle the season)
20. Sweet Sixteen album (for that special birthday/year)
21. Travel album
22. Best wishes/farewell album (for teachers or professional colleagues)
23. Graduation album
24. Mother's Day or Father's Day album

25. Teacher's/classroom album

26. Hobby/interests album

27. Friends and/or relatives album

28. "Welcome to the Family" album (for weddings, adoptions, and so on)

29. Recipe album (record family favorites for yourself or a child)

30. Brag book for Mom or Dad, Grandma or Grandpa

31. Garden album (include photos, details about favorite flowers, stories about your kids enjoying tomatoes or corn, and so on)

32. Arts or crafts projects album

33. Retirement album

34. "What I did on my summer vacation" album

35. Halloween album

36. "Thank you for your hospitality" album (include photos and stories from your visit)

37. Recovery (twelve-step)

38. Adoption album (chronicle child's journey to, and first year with, the family)

39. Niece/nephew/godchild album

40. Baby dedication/baptism/first communion/confirmation album

41. Teen album (document your teenager's high school and/or middle school years)

42. Landmark birthday album (forty, fifty, sixty, and so on)

43. Engagement album

44. Honeymoon album

45. New house, house construction, or remodeling album

46. Prayer or faith album (include photos of people you pray for and/or stories of everyday miracles and answered prayers)

47. Sisters/brothers album

48. Family reunion album

49. Affirmation album (filled with positive statements and photographs celebrating a person's good qualities)

50. Hunting, fishing, or camping album

look at them. Once they are in our laps, we often reminisce for the remainder of the evening. After we start talking about the pictures and stories, it's hard to stop. It's like eating potato chips: We want just one more. Just one more page, just one more story.

You'll Have a Source of Comfort

Life is filled with joyful moments—and difficult ones. When we are hurting, our albums can help us both cope and heal.

Rhonda, for example, had a mother who was extremely diligent about putting together albums for her family. As a result, when Rhonda was a girl, she had her very own albums to turn to in difficult times.

One of the most traumatic events in her life happened when Rhonda was eleven years old. That year her grandmother died. Rhonda had been particularly close to her grandmother, a wonderful woman who'd had a way of making Rhonda feel as though she were her favorite grandchild. After her grandmother's death, Rhonda found herself thinking, *Now that she's gone, what is my life going to be like?* Her mind full of worries, she turned to her photo album, where she found dozens of pictures taken by her parents: photos of Rhonda on the first day of school in her new school clothes; photos of Rhonda practicing her piano lesson and playing at her recital. Each picture reminded her how much she was loved. Rhonda realized that, even though her grandmother was not with her any more, she wasn't alone and there were still people who believed she was special.

Not long afterward, Rhonda had a very different reason to seek comfort in her albums.

Rhonda: We moved to Great Falls, Montana, when I was in the seventh grade. On my very first day at the new school, I saw that it was very different from what I was used to. It was huge, and I had always gone to a small school. There was a lot to adjust to!

Then that morning in my homeroom class, I saw a girl looking at me, and I heard her say to another classmate, "See that new girl over there? Let's *not* be friends with her!"

That year was a very difficult time for me, and I remember specifically relying on my photo album a lot. My album reminded me that I
did have friends. It reminded me that I *was* loved, that there were
places where I *did* belong.

Whether we are coping with the death of a loved one or seeking solace
during a difficult time, our photo albums can be for us a tremendous source
of comfort, strength, and encouragement.

START NOW—BEFORE IT'S TOO LATE

These are just a handful of the benefits you can receive from photo albums,
and we encourage you to start album making right away. We all have a lim-
ited time on this earth, and if we wait, it will eventually be too late for us—or
for those we love—to chronicle the important stories we want to share with
the next generation.

Every day, we at Creative Memories hear many stories about people who
waited too long—and about some who acted just in time. Not long ago, we
heard about a woman who realized that she had only one blurry photograph
of her brother to put into her album. Determined to get the photographs she
needed, she gave a disposable camera to her family to use when he visited
from out of state. As she had requested, her family took photographs of her
brother to send to her. On his way home from that visit, he was killed in an
automobile accident.

Obviously, nothing can lessen the tragedy of this man's death. Yet, his family was able to find some comfort in the photographs that would not have
been taken if it were not for his sister's determination to make a keepsake
album of her family.

People constantly tell us about how valuable their photographs truly are.
Just last week, our editor returned from a dream vacation in Portugal and
Spain—only to learn that the airline had lost her suitcase, which contained nineteen rolls of film from the trip. The bag included hundreds of dollars of clothes
and gifts. "But the worst of all," Liz mourned, "was the loss of those photos!"

Mary Lou Ungar reported seeing this sign while vacationing in Ocean City, Maryland:

> Lost: A Canon 35mm camera and black bag with Canon Logo. I DO NOT CARE ABOUT THE CAMERA! All I want returned is the film in the camera and the roll in the bag. Please return. No questions asked. $100 reward!

Thankfully, such losses are the exception, not the rule. Chances are, you have most—if not all—of the photographs you've treasured over the years. Now you need to *do* something with them.

So let's get started!

Chapter Three

OUT OF YOUR HEART AND ONTO THE PAGE

A journey of a thousand miles
must begin with a single step.
—CHINESE PROVERB

"Begin at the beginning," the King said, gravely,
"and go till you come to the end; then stop."
—LEWIS CARROLL, *Alice's Adventures in Wonderland*

In the 1998 comedy-drama romance *Hope Floats,* newly single mother Birdee Pruitt recounts for her daughter Bernice a nugget of wisdom passed on to her by her own mother. "Beginnings are scary," Birdee says. "Endings are usually sad. But it's the middle that counts the most."[1]

From first-day-of-school nerves to the anxiety of new parenthood, we've all experienced the fears that come with starting something new. We've also felt the loss that comes with endings, as well as the contentment, challenge, and joy found in between the two.

Creating a keepsake album is no different. At the beginning, the task can seem overwhelming, especially if you have stacks and stacks of photos that need to be placed in an album. But when you reach the end of an album or a page, you can feel a twinge of sadness. After all, when you are making a page—

poring over old photographs, rifling through your memories, weighing what
to write—you relive your past experiences, no matter how many times you
look at your favorite pages.

As you start making albums, however, you'll quickly move into the heart
of a process that will reap great rewards for you and your family. At times, you
may be tempted to give up or to second-guess your perfectly wonderful efforts.
Don't cave in. Don't give up!

TAKING THE FIRST STEP

At long last, you've decided to get those photos into albums. You're catching a
vision for creating your own life story and the story of your family. So where
do you begin?

In this chapter, we will share some of the basics that can get you moving
in the right direction. First, we'll walk you through the four steps of getting
organized. Then we'll share a few of the basics about getting your photos and
stories onto the page.

GETTING ORGANIZED

Step One: Collect

Find those elusive photos. First and foremost, you'll want to gather all your
photographs in one place. (If you're like most of us, this part will take a
little time, but remember that it's time well spent.) Where should you put
your photos once you start pulling them together? Any place—as long as
it's always the *same* place! Don't buy expensive storage containers. Remember what we told you about Rhonda and the top of her dishwasher? You're
only going to store your photos until you can get them into albums, which
can happen much faster than you might think. Use what you have on
hand—and be committed to moving your photos into albums as quickly as
possible.

Gather those keepsakes you've been saving for years. Along with your scattered
photographs, make sure you gather up and save your miscellaneous memorabilia: plane tickets, greeting cards, stickers, subway ticket stubs, holiday letters,

party invitations, birthday announcements, handwritten notes, and so on. These items can add a rich dimension to your albums. Remember, your albums are not just for photographs. This is your story! You can add whatever you want. Whatever is important to you, whatever might trigger an important or simply enjoyable memory, whatever might be of interest to your descendants a century from now ("The bank papers say she paid how much for her first house?")—these are the items you'll want to keep.

What Do I Do with My Negatives?

Your photo negatives are important, and we *strongly* suggest that you keep them. Someday you (or one of your descendants) may want to find and print a special photo taken years before.

Creating an organized negative file includes

1. keeping your negatives together,
2. keeping your negatives in some kind of order, and
3. labeling them for easy retrieval.

Use a simple, safe, accessible negative storage system that works for you. Without question, the safest place for your negatives is in a fire- and heat-resistant container. For optimum safety, you may consider keeping your negatives in a bank's safety deposit box. Ideally, you will keep your photographs and negatives in different locations (preferably not in the same house or apartment), so that if your albums are ever destroyed, you'll have your negatives with which to reconstruct them. You may also make color photocopies of your album pages for this same purpose. (Make sure you store those copies with your negatives.)

At the very least, try to put your negatives in a file box that can be located quickly in an emergency. We hope you will never need to rescue your negatives; but taking the precaution will not require a great deal of effort and could potentially save you a great deal of heartache.

Step Two: Decide

Next, you'll want to decide what type of album(s) to make. In the upcoming chapters, we'll talk about many different types of albums. Albums you may wish to start with include the following:

- *Heritage albums* are generally filled with old photographs that document your family history.
- *Family albums* chronicle your life and the lives of the people you lived with. These albums are organized by topic or by date.

Put Your Memorabilia to Work

- Add newspaper articles to your album by making a high-quality photocopy of the newsprint and storing the original in a cool, dark file.
- When adding greeting cards to your album, instead of storing the entire card, just cut out portions of it—the words *Happy Birthday,* a Snoopy cartoon, colorful flowers, or a personal note. This method conserves space on your page and spices up your album with color and variety.
- Don't forget to add other types of memorabilia: programs (plays, graduations, weddings, church events, and so on), ticket stubs (airlines, trains, buses, and subways, as well as movies and other events), pressed flowers, certificates, ribbons, awards, photocopies of newspaper articles and cartoon clippings, a wisp of hair from baby's first haircut, subway tickets or metro cards, a school ID, foreign currency, postcards, hotel/motel brochures, menus, receipts, admission tickets, maps, visitor's guides, magazine articles, and more.
- Anything that can trigger memories, help document your story, and fit into your album is fair game! (If something is too large or bulky for your album, consider taking a photograph of the item and including it in your album instead.)

- *Children's albums* come in a wide variety. For example, you may make a chronological album that covers your child's life, a topical album that includes character traits, or an album that focuses on his or her birth.
- *Tribute albums* are gift albums, created for someone important in your life to express your love or appreciation.
- *Celebration albums* are all about you and the people and things you care about most.
- *Thankfulness albums* are filled with photos and stories about the blessings you've received, your feelings about those gifts, and your beliefs about the source of those blessings.

Think about a possible focus for your album as you collect your photos. Look for the main themes in your photo collection. If it helps you to do so, list several different topics you might choose from, such as family, friends, vacations, or celebrations.

You cannot make a "wrong" choice. Each person's approach to an album is perfectly valid. The two of us, for example, have very different ways of approaching our albums.

Rhonda tends to work chronologically, and as mentioned earlier, she finds it personally satisfying to make photo albums for each of her kids. Because multiple family members frequently appear in a single photograph, she often has reprints made so that she can include the photo in each child's album. In addition to the children's albums, Rhonda also makes family albums. When the kids leave home with their personal albums, she and her husband will still have their own albums to remember and enjoy.

Cheryl, on the other hand, prefers to work topically. That simply works best for her. She has an album about her dogs, one about her motorcycle, and another full of special cards and notes from people she loves and who love her.

That's the beauty of this tradition. It's highly personal. Which is the "right" approach for you to take? Whichever one excites you the most! Whatever method brings you most quickly to your goal of completed albums—that's the one we recommend for you.

Step Three: Sort

Once you've decided on a specific album project, sorting will be easier than you think. You might choose to sort everything you have, or simply sort what you need for your first project.

Here are four popular categories for sorting photos and memorabilia that work well for album makers just starting out:

- *Big Events.* Any event that is monumental in your life can be considered a "big event": a vacation, a celebration, a graduation, holidays, or any other experience. When sorting your photos, use subcategories to separate them, such as: "Getting Ready for the Party," "The Party," and "Cleanup."

- *Chronology.* Definitely one of the easiest ways to sort photos, chronological order is achieved by simply identifying the approximate date of the photos or memorabilia, writing down the date, and placing the photos in order. Most of our parents used this method when we were growing up to create the family albums from our childhoods.

- *Family Members.* Would you like to have an album of photos of your recently departed mom? Do you wish you had a "brag book" of your new grandson? Dividing up your photographs by family members requires the greatest concentration and the most planning. You'll want to start by dividing your photo collection and ordering duplicates as needed. Then, you'll sort each group of photos chronologically.

- *Ancestry/Heritage.* Since ancestral photos represent family heritage, you will want to sort your photos into categories that will make the process of finding and recording stories as easy as possible. Sorting should begin with separating photos and memorabilia by family lineage: for example, your mother's family and your father's family. Then, you might want to break these broad categories down even further. You might, for example, want to group together all the photographs of your maternal grandmother's family. Finally, the next time you visit your mom's mother, you can take along those photographs and a notepad, and jot down notes while you ask your grandmother questions about her family.

Step Four: Commit to "Simple Pages, Completed Albums"

Remember the KISS method (Keep It Simple, Sweetheart). Resist the temptation to create "a work of art." *You* are the work of art. Your albums exist simply to tell your story. So, concentrate on what matters most: your photos and your stories. We've found that simple pages are the fastest and easiest way to completed albums.

What exactly are simple pages? They are pages that can be completed in about ten to twenty minutes each. They may be created with a pen and a few pieces of precut paper. They may include stickers or precut paper shapes known as diecuts. In some cases, the written word is the only embellishment on a page.

Whatever they include, simple pages guarantee that albums will be completed. They allow us to preserve stories that inspire us, educate us, and give us reason to celebrate. In years to come, we will know about the first wobbly ride after the training wheels came off the bike. We will see the snapshots and read about our sons stationed overseas. We will enjoy family reunion photos that put faces to the names from oral history that has been handed down. With completed albums, our lives can be more meaningful.

OUT OF THE SHOEBOXES, OUT OF YOUR HEART

Now that you've organized your photos and memorabilia, you're ready to start putting your photos and stories down on paper.

If you would like help getting started, we strongly encourage you to attend a Creative Memories Home Class or Workshop. There is absolutely no substitute for the kind of hands-on guidance you can receive from an experienced album maker or for the support you get from—and fun you share with—other participants who are starting out just like you.

For your convenience, we've included in the back of this book our Web site address and the phone number of our home office. If you would like, we would be delighted to match you up with a consultant in your area. Our Creative Memories consultants offer products, guidance, and encouragement every step of the way.

ONTO THE PAGE

Step One: Select

Start with eight to twelve photos of one specific event, along with any related memorabilia. You will draw from these to fill one or more pages. If you're starting with a topical or thematic album, choose one subcategory. If, for example, you're working on an album for your teenager, you may want to start with her junior prom. Then, break that even down even further and separate out the photographs of your daughter getting ready for the event (getting her hair done, doing her makeup with her friends, waiting for her date's arrival).

If you're working on a chronological album, we recommend starting with your most recent photos and working backward. It's much less intimidating than starting with your baby pictures and trying to work up to today! Simply start with your most recent batch of photographs, say, from your last fishing trip or your cousin's wedding. Include a copy of your fishing license or the program you saved from the wedding. Using memorabilia like that whenever possible will help bring your album to life.

Next, lay out your first album page (or pages). Try your photographs in different configurations. Decide if you want to add to or drop photographs from the mix. Consider how much journaling you would like to do. You may want to include one photograph on a page with a lot of journaling or five photographs with brief captions—or you may land somewhere in between.

You may choose to crop certain photographs (an empty couch cushion doesn't add much variety to a photo) or to cut away the background completely, following your subject's silhouette. Some people cut select photographs into circles, ovals, or other shapes. (You can purchase tools that will help you do this evenly. We have yet to see someone cut a perfect circle or oval freehand!)

When you're first starting out, it's a good idea to use duplicate photos when you're cropping or to cut only after you've confirmed that you have the photograph's negative. Perfection isn't necessary—but we've all had the experience of cutting off too much of someone's hair so it looks as if he or she is wearing a helmet, or of accidentally cutting a hand completely out of a photograph! At the same time, be gentle with yourself; don't make yourself do pages over and over again until you have them "just right." Barring disaster (such as cutting someone's head out of a photo), accept a page as completed and move on. Then you're one step closer to starting your *next* album!

Step Two: Mount

Once you've decided on your general layout, mount your photographs and memorabilia to the page. Make sure you use adhesives that are *safe* for your photographs and easy to use. Options include photo tape, photo mounting sleeves, and photo mounting corners. The adhesive used in these products is generally quite strong and doesn't release from a page easily (if at all). So once you've placed a picture, try to leave it in place and work around it. Appreciate what you've done. Enjoy it—and move on to the next step. You're making progress!

Step Three: Journal

When you have your photos and keepsakes on the page, it's time to add the words. *Do not skip this step!* The lyrics of an African folk song say that when an old person dies, it's as if a library has burned down. It is true. There's a richness of family heritage in each person's life that will be lost if it isn't recorded for the next generation.

You have the ability to do much more than brief, simple who-what-where-when captions. As we've said from the very beginning, *everyone has a story to tell.* Now is the time to get *your* story onto the page! We've listed three popular approaches to journaling:

- *Bullet journaling* includes the who, what, where, when and why. Details for the page can be written under each photo or grouped together in one spot. What you write is normally a list of words, descriptive phrases, or brief sentences that capture the main details of the event.
- *Quick captions and comments* allow you to reflect on what is happening in a photo and also tell why you took the photo. Often, captions or subtitles can set a mood or tone. They may also describe the thoughts and feelings of the pictures. Examples include quotations, anecdotes, or poems. These captions include longer comments and may be two or three sentences long.

• *Storytelling* is writing the facts or information about the event in paragraph form. This full account of the event captures more of the details. If you are writing from the heart and sharing special feelings, storytelling may well be your best option. Storytelling may range in length from a paragraph to a full page.

Give as much detail and share as many feelings as you can. Then keep moving on. You can always add more later! And as you learn, the process will become even easier.

Remember, every detail counts. We've heard mothers say, "I had three children, and now, when I look back at their baby pictures, I don't know which one's which!" You think you'll never forget. But, twenty years later, you see a photo of a little, baldheaded baby, and you wonder. It's hard to tell—they are all related, you know. So you find yourself asking, "Is that Bill or is that John?"

Bill and John will want you to know.

tip

But What Do I Write?

Here are just a few questions to nudge you in the right direction when you suffer from writer's block.

• Who is in the photo?
• What is happening in the photo? What were we doing that day?
• Where and when was the photo taken?
• Why is this loved one (or loved ones) important to me?
• What was the most interesting moment or most exciting event of this day?
• What is my favorite thing about what is shown in the photo (spring, Christmas, my birthday, and so on)?
• What little details (food served, games played) made this day special?
• What was our favorite quote (or quotes) of the day?
• What special bonds or connections were made?
• What do I most want to remember about this day?

Step Four: Enhance

Finally, add your own special visual touches: stickers, diecut shapes, and so on. Here is another opportunity to develop your own style. You may like just a few elements, or you may choose several embellishments. Either way, make sure your creative touches add to the story rather than detract from it. *You*—and not a teddy bear sticker—are the star of this show!

BUILD YOUR VISION

Now that you have some of the basics down, we're going to explore more specifically how your albums can help preserve the past, enrich the present, and inspire hope for your future.

In the following chapters, we hope that you will catch our vision of the power keepsake photo albums can have in people's lives. But more importantly, we hope that you will begin to develop your own vision of how making albums can impact *your* life. In a society that is hungry for meaning, albums can help build your family's sense of identity and togetherness. There will never be a better time to take advantage of your album-making opportunities. Everything you need is easily acquired or already at your fingertips.

KNOW YOUR STORY

In the film *Moulin Rouge,* a young poet named Christian (Ewan McGregor), the French courtesan, Satine (Nicole Kidman), and a group of quirky bohemian revolutionaries dream of staging the elaborate musical *Spectacular! Spectacular!* at the Moulin Rouge dance hall. In order to do so, they require a financier.

Enter the foppish English duke.

"What's the story?" asks the duke. "If I'm going to invest," he says quite reasonably, "I need to know the story."[2]

Like the duke, none of us wants to invest—money, time, energy, or heart—in an unknown story.

Many chapters in our lives can feel empty, overwhelming, even heartbreaking. At such times, it is crucially important that we know the greater story. Through words, pictures, and memorabilia, you can capture the heart of *your* story in all its messy, wonderful glory, so that you will not forget where you've been or lose sight of where you're headed.

In *Keeping a Journal You Love,* author Sheila Bender describes journal keeping as a "journey one takes by writing, day after day, in the hopes of finding better understanding and a fuller world."[3] In this and many other ways, album making is very similar to journal writing.

In an interview published in the U.K. edition of *Elle* just prior to *Moulin Rouge's* British premiere, McGregor admitted that he was glad to be back home after nine months of shooting the film in Australia. "That's a long time…you lose sight of friends, family; you lose the plot."[4]

At times, we all need to be reminded of the plot. That's what our albums do. They bring us back to heart of the story. To the middle. To the part that counts the most.

PART II

Preserving Your Past

We live in reference to past experience,
and not to future events, however inevitable.
—H.G. WELLS, *Mind at the End of Its Tether*

What's past is prologue.
—WILLIAM SHAKESPEARE, *The Tempest*

A man he seems of cheerful yesterdays
and confident tomorrows.
—WILLIAM WORDSWORTH, *The Excursion*

Chapter Four

WHO AM I AND
WHERE DID I COME FROM?

To forget one's ancestors is to be a brook
without a source, a tree without a root.
—CHINESE PROVERB

A good man leaves an inheritance
for his children's children.
—ANCIENT HEBREW PROVERB

Dr. James Dobson, family advocate and host of the syndicated radio program *Focus on the Family,* stated in his June 22, 2000, broadcast: "If there is anything that I feel we have lost as a people in the western world, it is that understanding of who we are, where we've been, who our ancestors were, what our identity is. That is done through the family structure. Continuity from generation to generation depends on taking the best from the past and passing it along to our children."[1]

Dr. Dobson isn't the first or only person to long for the comfortable anchor of yesteryear. According to trend tracker Faith Popcorn—who coined the phrase "cocooning" to describe the practice of withholding ourselves from the unpredictable realities of the outside world—more and more of us are "reaching back to our spiritual roots, taking what was secure from the past in order to be ready for the future."[2] Popcorn reports that we are turning back to our family genealogy for clues about living. Internet and software shelves are stocked with systems for tracking our ancestry, and genealogy Web site http://www.rootsweb.com gets 400,000 hits per day.[3]

Why are we experiencing this intense desire to connect with the past? Why this passion for the family tree? Maybe we sense that the past holds important insights for today as well as for our tomorrows. "The most important part [of this new trend called anchoring]," says Popcorn, "is taking comfort in what was safe and secure from the past in order to get ready for the future."[4] No doubt we've all learned a valuable lesson or two from the stories of those who raised us, from time- and life-tested wisdom about how to build a strong marriage to invaluable tips on everyday living like "never lick a metal fence post in the winter"!

Or perhaps we are searching for something deeper and more lasting than what much of this world has to offer. In a society that hungers for meaning, many of us are turning to the past for insights about life and love, faith, and identity. We look to our roots, hoping to find a genuine sense of belonging. We long to connect with our families, to "know" those who strolled or built the roads we walk, and to discover how their lives can speak to ours today.

At Creative Memories we, too, long to connect more deeply with the past. And one of the most effective ways we've found to do so is to create what we call a heritage album.

WHAT IS A HERITAGE ALBUM?

Like a chest filled with treasures, a heritage album shows who you are and where you came from. It chronicles the lives of your sisters, your brothers, your mom, your dad, their parents, their parents' parents, and countless subgroupings and spin-offs. It tells the stories of relatives you know well and ancestors you'll never meet in this lifetime. A heritage album is a place you can go when it feels like the world has gone crazy, and there you will find signs of good times and hope, of history and love. After all, it will be the product of endless conversations with those who know your family's story.

Your heritage album can include anything that links you to the past: sepia photographs, pages from an old diary, genealogy charts, the deed for family property, and stories—as many as you and your loved ones can commit to paper.

Your album may include details about the lifestyle of your ancestors, such as their occupations and their living conditions. It may relate details that seem outrageous to us today—stories of three brothers marrying three sisters or of a great-great-grandmother who birthed an astounding fourteen children. (What if she had stopped at thirteen? Would you still be here today? Would you still be you?) The album may include personal links to the past like notes about a namesake or photos of a distant cousin you resemble closely enough to have been a twin.

The album may also—and, whenever possible, should—include stories that lay bare your relatives' hearts: How did they think, what did they feel, what touched them deeply? Such details are key to the rich benefits you can reap when you create a heritage album: benefits like getting to know your family better, being assured that your family history will not be forgotten, helping your loved ones tap into their memories, and feeling connected with loved ones who have died.

Getting to Know—and Love—Your Family Members

Our friend Shari MacDonald, an avid album maker, never met her grandfather Earl. But she heard many stories about him while she was growing up. Her grandmother explained that when Earl came home from World War I, he seldom spoke about his tour of duty in Europe. Though his lungs had been turned leathery by mustard gas, causing him to struggle for breath throughout his life, he never complained and did not speak of the horrors he'd witnessed and experienced overseas.

Then one day, his wife came home from work to find Earl uprooting the neighbor's newly planted poppies.

"What are you doing?" she asked, incredulous.

"I *hate* poppies!" he said with uncharacteristic fierceness.

The reason? Earl had fought, and many of his comrades had fallen, at the poppy-covered battle site that inspired the famous poem by John McCrae, "In Flanders' Fields." Those flowers reminded Earl of the tragic deaths of his friends.

"I hate poppies." That one comment, and the manner in which it was spoken, told Shari much about her grandfather's feelings about the loss of so many of his friends.

Though Shari never met her grandfather, she learned to love him through stories like these and the conversations they sparked. She found that she was like him in many ways: They both were gentle, and they both hated war and the idea of killing. They both loved their country, even though they didn't always like what its leaders did. She learned that her grandfather loved people deeply and that he grieved terribly the loss of his friends. Through these connections, she came to love him and grieve for him, though she will never meet him in this life. And with his story safely chronicled in her album, Shari knows that her children's children will love him too.

Stories like these that have been passed down through the generations are often rich with emotion. Thousands of such tales remain untapped in the minds of those closest to us. All we need to do is ask for them.

Keeping Important Stories from Being Lost

There are specific things that each of us wants to know about our family. Perhaps you like knowing how many children your ancestors had. Maybe you are interested in genealogy or countries of origin. Rhonda likes to learn about her spiritual heritage.

> **Rhonda**: When I interview each of my relatives, I ask three questions: How did you meet your spouse and decide to marry? What were the major turning points in your life? What were your spiritual beliefs?
>
> My husband, Mac, tells the story about an ancestor who lived in Norway. One day, Mac's great-grandpa, Frederic, was on the street corner when he came across a Salvation Army missionary. He became a Christian right then and there. Then he went home and shared his faith with his wife, who also became a Christian. Shortly thereafter, they decided they wanted to go be missionaries in Madagascar. They applied to the missionary board for permission to go, but the board said (understandably), "You've got thirteen children. You really need

to stay at home and raise them." So they did. But they prayed for their children to become missionaries, and, incredibly, many of them did.

I love that story! It tells me what Mac's grandparents valued, and it shows how their beliefs shaped the lives of their children. My descendants will read that story and always know where their heritage of faith got started. It also helps build my faith in God—reminding me that he answers prayers and reassuring me that he is watching over me and my family.

Heritage albums can also help us learn things about our families that we would not have otherwise learned. Donna Haller told us this story: "A couple years ago my mother asked me to help her do an album. She said she wanted to tell the story of her first husband, Earl, for his grandchildren. Earl was killed in World War II and left behind a two-year-old daughter, my oldest sister.

"A year after the war, my mother married my father and had seven more children. We knew a little about Earl, but she didn't talk much about him out of respect for my father. Many of the stories my mother knew had never been told to anyone, and she was the last person living who could share them. She wanted my sister, her children, and now the next generation to know all about him.

"My mother began writing the stories in October and in a month had completed fifty handwritten pages. I typed them on the computer and laid out the twenty-five typed pages, photos, letters, and other memorabilia, rearranging everything to fit together. We copied the album three times—one each for my two nephews and niece—and my mother gave them as Christmas gifts that year. It was a very special gift not only for them, but for all of us. We learned more about my mother through those stories and gained respect for her because of what she had been through." That's not surprising, as you'll see from what Donna's mother wrote:

Then came the day that was to ruin our lives. It was Sunday, December 7, 1941. We had gone to church and then come home, and both of us were cooking dinner. [Friends] Albert and Wanda were coming over. I don't remember what time they came, but I'll never forget the looks on their faces when they got there. They asked if we had our radio on. When we told them we hadn't, they said, "Pearl Harbor has been bombed by Japan, and we are at war." I admit I wasn't sure where Pearl Harbor was, but we all knew what the word *war* would mean to all of us. If it had been Germany, no one would have been surprised because our whole country had been expecting to go to war with them. The news about Adolf Hitler's reign of terror was beginning to reach us regularly.

The effects of the war were indeed catastrophic, and Earl lost his life shortly after the birth of the couple's daughter.

Years later, while helping her mother sort through Earl's things, Donna found a box full of old postcards that showed pictures of different castles, each one bearing the name Valkenburg.

Use Your Time Wisely

You may be worried that you won't get your older relatives' stories down on paper while they are still around to tell them. But at the same time, you may be overwhelmed by the idea of getting all those stories onto paper *immediately*. Consider using one of these approaches:

- If your older relatives are still able to write, ask them to write down their favorite stories in their own handwriting. Have them look through your photos or photo album and write down their stories on acid-free paper, which you can later add to your album. Tell them that you want to have all their cherished stories, even if the stories don't correspond with a particular photograph.
- Use a tape recorder to capture the stories on cassette. Keep the cassettes even after you've transferred the stories into your album. That way, you'll have your loved ones' voices recorded for posterity as well.

"I said, 'What do you want me to do with these?' " Donna remembers. "My mother said, 'Oh, just pitch them. We don't know what they are.' I turned one of them over, and it said, 'Honey, be sure and keep these cards. Lots of love, Earl.' And we both just burst into tears because we knew that he wanted her to keep them so he could explain to her all about them. He just never got the chance. He had said in some of his letters that he was living in a castle somewhere; he wasn't allowed to say where. But, oh, it was just so sad that he never got to tell her what the postcards were of."

Today, Donna says, many people have read the album, but none have finished the story with dry eyes. The reason: "It could be the story of hundreds of young couples who lived during that time, and many people have been inspired to write their own story because of it.

"My mother became ill right after that Christmas, and she never would have been able to do the album if she had waited any longer. She passed away last Thanksgiving, but she left us the most wonderful gift—her memories."

Bringing Understanding and Healing

Few of us delve into our piles of photographs with the goal of finding healing. We simply want to get organized and find those countless pictures a home! Yet the process often blesses us in ways we never would have dreamed possible.

Several years ago, Marlys McDonald's mother, Mercedes Rinkel, came to visit. Her goal was to organize the six boxes of pictures she had accumulated in her eighty-seven years. For three months, the two women worked together on the project almost every night, filling two and a half albums.

During that time, Marlys and her mother had a wonderful time, laughing and sharing together. But Marlys also learned about important events from early in her mother's life—information that had a lasting impact on them both.

One evening, while Marlys was at work, Mercedes wrote in her album about the most pivotal event in her life, which had happened when she was sixteen years old:

My mother died at 4 A.M., and my world stopped.

My dad called me to come down, as Mama was very sick. She was sitting up in bed, propped against pillows and having trouble breathing.

And she said, "Marsada [the German version of *Mercedes*], I'm dying. And I know you will take care of Ed and Allie" [pronounced "Ollie"; Mercedes's younger brothers].

I cried and said, "I can't." And she just looked at me. By that time, Allie woke up and came down, crying. She said, "Take him back to bed," which I did. And by the time I got him back to sleep, she was gone.

That was the worst day of my life. Everything that ever happened to me after that, I could handle.

Marlys says that her relationship with her mother deepened after that revelation. She had never heard that story before, and now she knows her mother better. She understands the pain and the drive to provide for her siblings that shaped her life. As a result, she feels even greater compassion and respect for her mother.

Mercedes, too, was changed by the experience. "It helped my mother's grieving process," Marlys says. "All those years, she had carried that experience with her. But writing it in the album really put it in perspective. It was very therapeutic for her. She released a lot of it by writing it. That is when I noticed a change in her. She didn't dwell on her mother's death much after that."

If you already have stories like these about your relatives (and most of us do have some), *write them down!* Alone, you cannot possibly share all your stories with everyone whose lives might be impacted by them. By writing down these stories, you will expand your influence, ensuring that your words will reach those you love throughout your life—and beyond.

Feeling Connected with Your Loved Ones

As a senior in high school, Kristin Thomson made the momentous decision to attend Texas A&M University despite the fact that a large portion of her family, including her beloved Uncle Don, had attended A&M's rival school, the University of Texas. From that day on, Kristin and her uncle ribbed each other good-naturedly about the outcome of the annual football game between the two schools. The game was played over Thanksgiving, so the loser could expect to receive a joke gift at Christmas.

Luckily for Kristin, A&M was on a winning streak throughout her college years. But every winning streak must come to an end, and when it did, Uncle Don arrived at the family's Christmas celebration decked out in University of Texas colors: burnt orange and white. Many photographs were taken and, as was the custom in their family, Kristin's uncle signed a special page in her album.

The following May, Uncle Don passed away suddenly. As she left for the funeral, Kristin grabbed her album, knowing it contained some of the last pictures taken of him. When she arrived at his home, Kristin took out the album. To her delight, there, on the last sign-in page, was Uncle Don's signature followed by the University of Texas battle cry, "Hook 'em, Horns!"

"My rival," she says, "had gotten the last word!"

Those photographs of her uncle, his signature, and his playful "parting shot" will warm Kristin's heart every time she views that page.

Though neither Kristin's nor Mercedes's albums would strictly be categorized as heritage albums, they will be someday. The contemporary, chronological, or thematic albums you and I create today will be our grandchildren's heritage albums tomorrow.

GETTING THE STORIES

Rome wasn't built in a day, and neither will your albums be. You have more than one lifetime worth of history to get caught up on, so be gentle with yourself. Don't expect to get it all done overnight. If you push yourself too hard, you'll take all the fun out of the experience and burn out. *Then* how many albums do you think you'll get done?

That said, we cannot emphasize enough the importance of starting right away. Keeping the following points in mind can help ensure that you complete your albums.

Do the Work in Stages

Don't think that a two-week time period is going to magically present itself to you. It won't happen—and it doesn't need to. Capture individual stories as opportunities arise: during your weekly telephone conversation with your mother, for example, or on a spur-of-the-moment visit to your Aunt Martha's. If you have only thirty minutes, capture what you can during that amount of time. Jot down notes, bring a tape recorder, or use your computer (desktop and telephone at home, laptop in person). When the visit is over, store your notes in a safe place and transcribe them into your album as soon as possible while your memory of them is still fresh. When you're ready, do a little bit more work on your album. Then some more. Craft your life story one tender, enlightening, or unbelievable anecdote at a time.

Interview Relatives at Family Reunions

Even those of us who adore our families can find family reunions draining. It takes energy to connect with so many different people, some of whom may be virtual strangers. It's not easy to listen to stories about people you don't know and, frankly, may never even have had a desire to know! But family gatherings take on a whole new meaning when you are on a mission to gather stories for your albums. Distant aunts, long-lost cousins—each person is a potential source of information. You may be surprised by the stories you get—and by the fun you have in tracking them down!

Fill in Those Blanks

Not everyone knows enough about family history to put together a family heritage album. Donna Sherman has a suggestion:

Start by putting your photographs into an album, leaving enough space on each page for additional journaling.

Include a pen and some stick-on notes along with an invitation to family members to write any information they can provide regarding particular photos or family members. The completed notes can either be stuck onto pages where related photos appear or attached to the inside front cover.

Display the album at family events so you can gather information that you've never known before.

One year at a family reunion, while on a mission to gather stories, Fran Lawler gathered together the "great generation" in her family—the five living members of the original ten aunts, uncles, and their spouses—plus a few others who were old enough to appreciate stories of the "old days." Then Fran and her cousin Linda began to ask them questions.

"The aunts and uncles shared their lives with us: growing up during the Depression, their young adult days during World War II, the dating years, and the early years of their marriages. We were taken back in time, listening intently to their tales of dancing away at the Palladium with the big bands or going to a movie via streetcars for ten cents a ticket. We were taken back in time to the days when our parents were young and full of life.

"We were able to hear from five perspectives. They shared the pain of their father abandoning them as well as the joy of Christmas and the Fourth of July—the most celebrated holidays in their youth. And then there were the Halloween pranks played by the boys: taking off neighbors' gates and laying them against their fences, breaking the streetlights, getting caught. I saw yet another side of my dad who passed away four years ago!"

Such moments are magical—and can make you long for more.

"Our reunions had never lasted so late into the evening," Fran recalls, "but no one was willing to break the spell. It was as though all of us had been transported back into another era, surrounded by the people we have loved our whole lives. By the time we were saying our good-byes, we were all vowing to meet again next year and continue the stories at the point that these young couples had us."

Write Down the Stories—Even if You Don't Have Any Photos

Of course, not all of us have family photos that we can use to create a heritage album, and not every story will have a corresponding photograph. But there's no reason for that to slow us down! Last year, we heard about a woman who helped a friend who'd immigrated to this country with only one picture of his family. Because of the war, every other photograph this man had owned was lost.

His friend, an avid album maker, decided to help him put his family story down on paper to be treasured along with his one picture. Before long, the project grew—and, in time, several family members were reunited as a result.

Remember That It's Never Too Late to Start

"My grandmother, Kathryn Baugh, has saved every picture and obituary of almost everyone she has known in her life," reports Kelly Henry. Determined to see her grandmother's stories preserved, Kelly suggested that her grandma write with a photo pencil on the back of all the photos—some of which dated back to the 1800s. Kelly also gave her grandmother a high-quality keepsake album, hoping that she might even put the photos inside.

Kelly could not do the work herself, and her mother didn't know who some of the relatives were in the photographs. Carefully, Kelly explained to her

A Taste of Good Times

Worried about losing those favorite family recipes? Make them a part of your heritage album—or create an album just for them.

Lois R. Johnson's mother was killed in a car accident when Lois was a teenager, and Lois missed the opportunity to learn how her mother made special family recipes because they were not written down. This loss motivated Lois to pass along family recipes to her daughter in a distinctive way: She created a heritage cookbook.

Lois made a template of a chef's hat in three sizes and started writing the recipes on the chef's hats or other diecut paper shapes. On each page, she includes one recipe and a photo of the person who gave it to her, of herself preparing the dish, or of an event where people are eating the food. Her journaling includes a story about the recipe and where it came from, possibly a memory of preparing it for an occasion, and comments about how to serve it or what people said.

Make a list of five people in your family who can pass family recipes on to you. Call them and ask them to start collecting their favorites. Borrow one collection at a time and copy them onto anything you want: decorated recipe cards, simple index cards, or paper that has been cut using your own template of a chef's hat, dinner plate, stove, or other shape. Don't forget to ask your loved ones for a story to go with each recipe!

grandmother the importance of journaling, emphasizing how much she and her children valued the family stories.

To Kelly's delight, her grandmother—in her mid-eighties—began making albums and journaling.

"After completing a few pages, she suffered a stroke, and I thought I would be finishing the album for her," Kelly says. But her grandmother recovered and has gone on to complete her first album—and begin a second!

When she read the completed album, Kelly burst into tears. "Her journaling is wonderful!" she says. "I have shared this story ever since because I want people to know you are never too old to preserve your heritage, and life is too short to wait. No one can tell your stories like you can!"

MORE THAN THE PAST

As you see, creating a heritage album does more than house your ancestors' photographs. It helps you understand who you are and where you come from. It allows you to connect deeply with the past. It builds bridges between you and those who have gone before you, preserves priceless stories for future generations, and fosters deeper, healthier connections between loved ones.

This concept may be foreign to you. Like countless others, you may look upon your albums as possessions. We encourage you to view your albums as gifts you *experience*. Think of them also as keys. Keys that open doors to insight, truth, and a richer life today—and tomorrow. Keys to fuller understanding of yourself and appreciation for all who have contributed to your life. Keys to a richer, fuller future.

While your parents or other relatives are still with you, capture every precious story and identify the faces in every faded photograph you can. No matter what details you uncover, you'll see evidence that shows you're an important part of a larger community, a part of a lasting legacy.

Start this month, this week, or today! Scribble down a story, phone a relative to learn more about some family history, or sort and linger over a single drawer of photographs. You'll never regret the time you spend connecting with the past. But you'll almost certainly regret letting even a single story slip away.

You have nothing to lose—and more than a lifetime's worth of memories to gain.

Make a Date

What older relative have you wanted to connect with—or avoided because you don't know what to talk about? Who among your family might have stories they long to share—or stories they have never shared before? Think of one person and schedule a visit or make a phone call tonight! Make a list of several people in your family tree and focus on one at a time. Ask your grandfather, "What was your oldest sister like? How did she fall in love with her husband?" or "What are some things you remember best about your father?"

Or focus on your grandfather himself: "What was the world like when you grew up?" "Which of your parents are you the most like—and why?" "What's the strangest job you ever held?" and the ever-popular "What did you think when you first saw *me?*" (It's perfectly okay to focus on yourself a little bit too.)

Now make a list of familiar family stories you want to capture on paper and another list of people you don't know much about (such as your grandfather's siblings) and details you'd like to get (like where your grandmother got the picture frame you inherited).

To help you get started, here are a few questions you may consider:

1. Do we have any relatives who died in a war? What happened to his or her family?

2. What did Grandpa (or Great-grandpa) do in the war? Where did he serve?

3. When did our family first immigrate to the United States? What made them leave the country where they were born? Ask for details.

4. Do you know of any relatives who were artistic (or athletic, interested in academics, religious, musical, and so on) like me?

5. What is your favorite family story about my mother/father?

6. In what ways do I remind you of you (or of grandma, grandpa, and so on)?

7. Which of your grandmother's/grandfather's character traits do you see in my kids?

8. How did your parents meet? Please tell me the story of how they fell in love and got married.

9. What is the best family love story you have heard?

10. What are all the different jobs you (or your mother or father) have had? What was your favorite job, and why was it your favorite? What was the strangest job you ever had? the best?

11. What did you want to be when you grew up? What did your parents want you to do—and why?

12. What was your (or another relative's) greatest regret in life?

13. What was your biggest dream?

14. What is your favorite memory from growing up?

15. What would people be surprised to learn about you? about your mother, father, grandmother, and so on?

16. What was the most pivotal event in your life?

17. What was the best Christmas you ever had, and why was it the best?

18. Tell me about the house where you grew up. Did you have a special place there?

19. What was the funniest thing you ever did to your siblings (or cousins, neighbors, or friends)? What was the funniest thing they did to you?

20. What is your favorite family story?

These questions are just a few options. Get out a notebook and come up with a few of your own! Keep adding to it as questions come to you.

Chapter Five

PRESERVING YOUR CHILD'S HISTORY

How dear to this heart are the scenes of my childhood,
When fond recollection presents them to view.
—SAMUEL WOODWORTH, *The Old Oaken Bucket*

Tell it to your children,
and let your children tell it to their children,
and their children to the next generation.
—*Holy Bible*

For decades, many of us—parents, teachers, and others—have drawn inspiration and wisdom from a celebrated and widely circulated poem by Dorothy Law Nolte, originally published in 1954 in a local Southern California newspaper as part of Nolte's weekly column on creative family living. In "Children Learn What They Live," Nolte highlights the effects of positive influences such as encouragement, praise, recognition, acceptance, approval, security—as well as the effects of numerous negative influences—on the lives of children.[1]

Her poem states clearly a principle most of us have long suspected, but may not have articulated: When we fill our children's lives with positive feedback, we instill in them favorable characteristics and teach them desirable behaviors. When we offer our children negative input, we do exactly the opposite—to our children's detriment.

As parents (or aunts, uncles, grandparents, teachers, or other concerned adults), we know we have a profound influence on the young people we love. We have a tremendous responsibility to care for them. We also have a great opportunity to instill in our kids the qualities and skills they will most need in life. Each of these traits, of course, must be taught first and foremost through daily, face-to-face interactions: As you praise your teenage daughter for taking out the garbage without being asked, you teach her important lessons about appreciation. When you sit on the end of the bed, offering encouraging words to your son about his upcoming jazz band audition, you instill in him a sense of confidence. But, wonderfully, many of the things children need to learn—encouragement, praise, acceptance, approval, recognition, security—can also be passed on purposefully, consistently, and proactively through the creation of fun, child-friendly photo albums.

WHAT KIND OF ALBUM SHOULD I MAKE?

We can affirm and teach our children through our albums in several ways. In chapter three, we discussed a number of options for album makers. We've found that most parents generally begin by: 1) creating family albums (which can be organized by date or theme) and/or 2) creating individual albums (also chronological or topical/thematic) for each child. These albums may include duplicate pages from the family photo album or pages created especially for one child. (You might choose to add copies of the pages to the family album.)

We also recommend creating ABC albums for each child. These are perfect not only for small children, but also for teens and adults. In an ABC album, the theme of each page centers around a specific letter of the alphabet. Each letter may stand for an object (as in, for a baby, "Ellie loves **Apple**-sauce!"), a favorite literary quote, or a verse of sacred text.

Rhonda: In an ABC album I created for my oldest daughter, I put the following verse on the L page: "Like cold water to a weary soul is good news from a distant land."[2] This verse is important to me and to Janetta because of an experience I had at the time she joined our family.

Our family had been waiting to hear news about our first soon-to-be adopted baby. When you adopt babies from India, you just don't know when they're going to come. You simply get a phone call, and the agency says, "Your baby's on the way."

We hadn't heard a single word for several weeks. But the morning I read that verse, I thought, *Lord, does that mean that we're going to hear today about Janetta's arrival home?* At 4:30 that afternoon the phone rang. It was the adoption agency saying Janetta was coming. That story is a big part of her history. It shows her how eager we were for her to be a part of our family and how we looked forward to and anticipated her coming.

Don't be too literal when creating an ABC album. Rhonda could have written: "Like cold water to a weary soul is good news from a distant land" under C or W just as easily as L. You have lots of flexibility (a good word to use for your X page!). You can even use favorite sayings of family members. When asking what kind of ice cream his grandkids wanted, Rhonda's grandpa used to say, "Do you want white, plain, or vanilla?" Lines like these are another fun alternative to using famous quotes or verses! You could also include pictures of your child's favorite characters from books and cartoons.

ABC albums are a great, easy way to start album making, because you are working within the framework of the letters of the alphabet. You only have to come up with twenty-six verses, words, or themes; twenty-six pictures; and twenty-six stories. It's easy to think, *I can do this.*

Make Your Calendar—or Day Planner—Your Friend

Do you have trouble keeping the order of your photos straight or remembering what happened when? Here's a tip from Kimber Lybbert: "I keep a large calendar on my kitchen wall. On it, I jot down things the kids say or details about the picture I just took. Then when the photos are developed I don't have to spend a lot of time trying to figure out the significance or sequence of each picture."

Whether you create family, individual, or ABC albums, the benefits your kids will reap from their completion are immeasurable. We could probably write an entire book on that subject! But in our experience, the myriad benefits generally fall into two categories: 1) building our children's self-esteem and instilling a sense of significance, and 2) giving our children a sense of belonging and place in the family.

BUILDING SELF-ESTEEM
AND INSTILLING A SENSE OF SIGNIFICANCE

Noted child psychologists and adoption specialists have long stressed the importance of building self-esteem in our children. Our kids need to know emphatically that they are loved apart from their behavior, good or bad, and apart from any circumstances happening around them. They need to know that they are special and unique. Preserving their photos in an album is one highly effective way to build that sense of significance and self-esteem.

In her book *Dr. Toy's Smart Play: How to Raise a Child with a High PQ* *Play Quotient,* Stevanne Auerbach lists scrapbooking as one of 160 affirming, self-esteem building play ideas parents can enjoy with their children.[3] Self-esteem is crucial, Dr. Auerbach says, because children "develop their basic feelings of value from their parents. When they feel they are important and valued, they are later able to move out of the home into other relationships with a greater sense of security about themselves."[4] An increased ability to trust, the ability to expand and deepen relationships, and greater achievement in school are among the many benefits of healthy self-esteem.

So how do family photo albums help build these skills? Simply put, the creation of the albums demonstrates to your children that you cared enough to record the specific details of the big and small events in their lives. "The child feels a sense of the importance of themselves to their parents and their role in the family," says Auerbach. "That builds their feelings of self-esteem and a feeling of value." It also provides a trigger for those feelings by cataloging "special times and events that are great to review later."[5]

Dianne Rohwer-Johnson's three-year-old grandson, Buddy, spent a memorable night at her house. They sat on the couch and read a bedtime story.

When the book was finished, Buddy asked to read another book. Dianne told him, "Nana does not have any other little boy books."

"Yes, you do," Buddy replied. He ran down the hall into the room where Dianne keeps her supplies and albums. He pointed to his baby album and said, "Here! This is my favorite book in the whole wide world!"

"My heart swelled, and my eyes filled with tears," Dianne says. "It was then I knew for certain that the albums I am creating will be treasured for a lifetime!"

As a divorced mother of three, Deb Yagel works full-time and supports the activities of all her children, including athletics (she claims they have all sports covered), the prom committee, church commitments, and more. At first, Deb was simply looking for a decorative way to display her photos, but she discovered something more significant.

"What I found," she says, "is not an obsession with a cut-and-paste craft, but another way I can strengthen that family bond between my children. Words can't express the joy it brings me to see them huddled around an album, sharing memories of learning to ride a bike, sleepovers, summer camps, proms.… Our albums give my children a sense of unity that I strive so hard to keep, despite my divorce. It also strengthens the mother-child relationship because my children know that I have put an enormous amount of time and planning into each of their albums. More than that, it gives them a sense of individuality—the feeling of really being their own special, unique person— because it shows them that that's exactly what they are."

Just having a book that's about them feeds our children's souls. Yet we can multiply our impact when we include pages that focus on key moments and memories in our children's lives.

Catch Your Kids Being Good

In his legendary *Dr. Spock's Baby and Child Care,* Dr. Benjamin Spock reflects on his experience of being raised by a critical mother. "As a child," he writes, "I was so often reprimanded for 'naughty' acts that every time I came home from playing or from school I felt a cloud of guilt over/on my shoulders. 'What have I done wrong?' I would wonder, when actually I had rarely done anything wrong. I was a goody-goody."[6] He goes on to suggest that the key to instilling healthy self-esteem in a child is simply not to tear down a child's natural self-assurance. We like to take that one step further.

When Rhonda's kids were little, they used to get stickers in Sunday school that said, "Caught being good." What a great concept! So many times we catch people at their worst in life, but how often do we recognize those wonderful, everyday victories?

Think about the character traits or qualities you most value. Then make a special point of watching for those traits or qualities in your kids and documenting them in your albums.

Rhonda, for example, keeps a list of character qualities that she looks for in her kids. She watches for opportunities to capture those, and she makes a big deal about them in her photo albums. Here is just a partial listing of some of the character traits Rhonda looks for—and finds—in her children: compassion, contentment, gentleness, gratitude, honesty, humility, authenticity, conviction, discernment, faith, purity, fairness, generosity, wisdom, creativity, originality, mentoring, able to listen well, teachability, dreamer, and a love for God.

With this list in mind, Rhonda created a special page for her son Joel. The heading on the page is simply, "Faithful." The idea for this page came easily. Joel is a swimmer, and his sport requires a great deal of self-discipline. Every morning, he has to be at school by six. He has to swim and lift weights for two hours before school. After school, he swims for a couple more hours, and he needs to go to Saturday practices as well as swim meets. The amount of discipline required to accomplish all this would be a lot for an adult to manage, and Joel is still a teenager. Yet he has remained faithful, and Rhonda recognizes this character trait in her albums.

On the "faithful" page, Rhonda has included photographs of Joel swimming and a list of behaviors he has demonstrated, such as working hard and showing a positive attitude. She also included a quote from the coach: "Joel contributed to the team spirit by how he encouraged others." Joel also received the "Athlete of the Year" award from his school, so Rhonda wrote: "This new award was to be given to the swimmer who worked hard, demonstrated a positive attitude, improved his performance, contributed to team spirit, and swam well. What a joy it was to see Joel given this award to honor his faithfulness."

Faithfulness. Hard work. A spirit of encouragement. What would you include on your list of qualities to watch for in your kids? What would be different from Rhonda's list? What would you like to add? Take a few minutes to start your own list. Keep it someplace convenient—like in your checkbook or next to your computer—and add to it as ideas come to you. Then find a small notebook and record the moments that illustrate these traits being lived out by your children. Once you start looking, you'll be surprised at how many reasons you'll find to praise your kids!

Not only can you document your children's positive character traits, but you can also use your albums to show them that you recognize and value their strengths and accomplishments. All of us, but especially kids, desire to be recognized for our achievements. Kids need to know that they are gifted, that they are successful, and that the adults in their lives believe in them. As you fill the pages of your family album and your children's albums with encouragement and recognition, you are certain to have a significant impact on each child's heart.

Proclaim Parenting Pride

It is hard to imagine a parent who is *not* proud of his or her child's accomplishments. Yet some of us are certainly better than others at expressing that pride. By writing down your feelings for your child, you can grant the approval your child so desperately needs—now and in the years ahead.

"I never really understood the impact of keepsakes until my mother died in January 1998 from cancer," Mike Nistler told us. "My mother was a very private person, one who would never brag about herself or—heaven forbid—her children. Therefore, it was difficult for my mom to praise her offspring.

"More than a year after my mother died, my siblings and I decided it was time to inventory her belongings. Most we would donate. The mementos we would distribute among her children and grandchildren.

"As I was going through the contents of her dresser drawers, my jaw dropped when I came to her stash of newspaper clippings from my journalism career. Dumbfounded, I pulled column after column from this wooden treasure trove.

"Tears came to my eyes as I thought about my mom reading these columns and thinking enough of them to clip them out and store them away.

I wondered how many times she pulled open those dresser drawers and reflected on those columns—columns she could not and would not compliment me on. There is no journaling or narrative with any of these items. I can only guess about the significance and the stories that go with each. I wish she had been able to put into words—either spoken or written—what those mementos meant to her.

"That experience has strengthened my resolve to begin preserving not only my photographs, but my words. Someday my daughters will be able to read my thoughts instead of having to guess what they were."

How often do you tell your child, "I'm proud of you"?

How often do you write it?

Now is the time to begin.

---

tip

Caught in the Act

Here are just few ideas of "good" activities you can watch for in your child's life:

- taking time to talk to his or her grandmother (documented with words, a photo of them together, or possibly a recent birthday card from Grandma)
- earning a gold star on a paper (with either the paper itself included in the album or a photo of your child with the paper)
- cleaning up his or her room without being told (with a photo of your child in action)
- being nice to her little sister (maybe with a little poem about sisters)

How can you catch your child being good in the weeks and months ahead? Make a list of activities or traits you'll be watching for—and add to that list all week long!

As you catch your child being good, you may never appreciate your child more. More importantly, your child may feel more appreciated—and loved—than ever before.

GIVING A SENSE OF BELONGING
AND PLACE IN THE FAMILY

Every child longs to know that he or she has a special place and plays an important role in the family.

At some point in their lives, most kids begin to question: *Is there a reason I was born? Why do I exist?* These are serious questions that we all eventually ask. Thankfully, most of us are able to work through these questions in a way that allows us to keep moving forward—sometimes struggling, sometimes full of joy. But not everyone is so fortunate. Every year, an increasing number of people commit suicide, in part because they are convinced there is no reason to live.

According to the American Academy of Child and Adolescent Psychology, suicide is now the third leading cause of death for fifteen- to-twenty-four-year-olds and the sixth leading cause of death for five- to-fourteen-year-olds in the United States.[7] Certainly there are many factors behind this trend, including, in many cases, clinical depression or other issues. We are not suggesting that album making alone can prevent serious problems for young people who need psychological or medical intervention. Yet we cannot help but wonder how things might be different if *every* child had an album that proclaimed the message of his or her tremendous value. Remember what Rhonda's attorney friend said: *Everyone needs to have albums like these.* This is every bit as true for our children as it is for us as adults—perhaps even more so. Here are some ways that you can give your kids a sense of belonging.

Document Your Child's Arrival in Your Family
We often teach people who are putting together baby albums to share the stories of when and how they decided to have a child, and to include such details as offered prayer or other circumstances surrounding the pregnancy. What were Mom and Dad's jobs before baby came along, and what was going on in the family before the newest child was born? We often forget to record those kinds of details, but they will always be meaningful to our children.

But babies aren't the only children who join families. If you've adopted an older son or daughter, gained a stepchild, or cared for a foster child, you can create an album to welcome and celebrate that child's presence in the family.

JoEthel Griffin recalls that when she first started making albums, she began with two projects: a baby album for her youngest daughter, Hannah, and an album for her oldest daughter, Elizabeth's, third birthday. "During this time," she says, "my stepdaughter Ayrial would mention, in passing, that she wanted an album." So JoEthel provided one for her stepdaughter to work on. But since Ayrial was with them only on weekends, when errands and activities were generally planned, she was only able to complete a page or two.

At that time JoEthel got a great idea. "As Ayrial's sixteenth birthday was approaching," she says, "I got inspired to create an album for her that captured her first year of life. I felt she needed something that would truly give her a sense of her importance to our family."

As JoEthel compiled the album, she focused on photographs of Ayrial with both her mom and dad, feeling that it was important for Ayrial to see pictures of her family, together and unified. She also included a number of pictures of Ayrial's paternal grandmother, who had since passed away.

---

tip

Take Photos of the First Day of School

Many people take photographs of their children on the first day of school. You can chronicle your children's growth by taking this tradition one step further: photographing them on the first and last day of school. Take your photographs in the same spot, so you can see how your child has grown.

In the September 1, 1999, issue of *The Oregonian,* in the "It Works for Us" column by Tom McMahan, reader Dana Wimmer wrote: "I have my two daughters stand in the same spot as the fall picture dressed in the same clothes they wore on the first day of school. It's always fun to see how short the leggings and arms sleeves have become, how the hair has changed, how many teeth have fallen out, etc., in just nine months' time! Mark your June calendar now, so you won't forget."[8]

Even if your kids are already in school, you can begin this tradition this year. It's never too late to start!

On Ayrial's big day, JoEthel completed the album, placing the last sticker while sitting in the parking lot at Ayrial's Sweet Sixteen birthday party. JoEthel kept the album with her until the end of the party. Then she watched as Ayrial opened the box and, seeing the words and lovingly arranged photographs that captured her life, began to cry.

It is important to remember that the youngest children are not too young to look at pictures of themselves. And even the coolest teens need to know how much they are valued and loved.

Celebrate Each Child's Place in the Family

Are you an oldest child? The baby? A middle kid? Were you the responsible child in your family? Or were you the "clown"? Even as an adult, you continue to identify, negatively or positively, with the positions and roles you played in your family while growing up.

Your children, too, love to know how they fit into the family and its story. Whether their special gifts and talents, the traditions they've started, or the activities they've introduced to the family are mentioned, they enjoying seeing the impact they've had on their parents and siblings.

It is vital that we communicate to our children their key role in the family. So Rhonda fills her children's albums and their family albums with affirming messages like, "We appreciate you, Joel. You make us laugh!" and "Thank you, Jacob, for the amazing mechanical talents you share with us." She makes an effort to acknowledge who her kids are and express to them how much she and her husband Mac value them.

Adopted children, in particular, can benefit from knowing their place in the family. Dr. Auerbach suggests that the simple act of choosing photos and other memorabilia can be helpful to a child. As children experience what it means to purposely choose a photo or sticker, they can learn what it means to choose something because they want it: This will drive home the message that their parents, too, purposely chose *them* because they are an important, needed element of the family "page."

Tracy Kiefer recalls how the album she created for her newly adopted son, Ian, helped him transition into his new family.

"I felt it was important to bring to Ian images from his soon-to-be home when my husband Mike and I went to Romania to pick him up," she says. "So before we left, I put together an album for him showing all of our immediate family." That album was filled with head shots of Mike, Tracy, Ian's new cousins, and other close family members. On the front page of the album was the picture of Ian that the adoption agency had sent to the Kiefers.

Though Ian was only three years old and did not yet speak English, during the week that Mike and Tracy were in Romania, he learned all of the names of his new family in the album. (Uncle Brian was his favorite.) Ian carried the album everywhere. When the Kiefers got back to Minnesota, their new son kept it with him and would refer to it often.

"It helped him tremendously with the transition to his new life with us," Tracy remembers. In fact, for six weeks following his arrival in the States, Ian was still "reading" his book every night before bed.

All around the world, parents are testifying to the truth that albums are instilling in children a deeper, richer sense of belonging and place. Do you want your child to feel an even stronger connection to your family? Start an album for him or her today.

---

tip

What a Day!

Every baby's day of birth is special, but Joyce Anderson has an idea for making it especially memorable. She took a newspaper from the day of her son's birthday, made copies of selected portions, and included them in his book. The newspaper selections provide a historic perspective of what was happening in the world when her son was born.

If your baby is on his or her way, ask a friend to pick up and save the local newspaper (or papers) the day your child is born.

If you are creating an album for a child who was already born, visit your local library and ask how you can get access to and make copies of newspapers from his or her birth date.

Provide an Outlet for Your Child's Feelings

Few children actually are thrilled at the prospect of keeping a journal. But as every parent knows, children love stickers. Kids also love photographs of themselves. In fact, they love stickers and photos so much that they're willing to write about their feelings and stories if it means that they can get their tiny hands on them!

Gretchen Tarpley, who leads album-making workshops for kids, works with nearly fifty second through seventh graders each month.

"What I teach a lot is 'Tell it in *your* words,' " she says. "I spend very little time correcting spelling or grammar. But I spend a lot of time encouraging them to put down more information or to expand on ideas. If they have a photograph of their dog who died, I ask, 'What happened? How did you feel when it happened?' With another photo I ask, 'How did you feel when your best friend moved away?' "

You may find success in prompting your kids with similar questions. But if you still have difficulty getting them to cooperate, you can always follow Gretchen's example.

"I tell them all the reasons why journaling is important," she says. "Then I don't let them have their stickers until they do it!"

Capture Moments of Affection and Love

As parents, we want our children to know how much they are loved. We want them to have concrete proof that they can look back on during those times when they might doubt our love or when they might doubt themselves. We can provide them with that concrete proof in the form of the albums we lovingly create for them.

> **Rhonda:** In my daughter Janetta's photo album is a photograph of her with her dad at suppertime. Janetta didn't even notice she was doing it, but that night she sat through the whole meal with her arm around Mac's neck. She was practically choking the guy! I snapped that shot as a reminder of what has become a common sight in our house: I can't count how many times the two of them have sat together like that, demonstrating the love between father and daughter. If there is ever a

moment in the future when Janetta wonders, *Do my parents love me? Does my dad care for me? Did I care for him?* she can look at that picture and say to herself, *Yeah, look. I sat at mealtimes with my arm around his neck. I love my parents, and I wasn't afraid to show it.*

By capturing such moments, we not only create a record of the lives we share as families, but we also provide a lasting testimony of how much we love our children…a testimony that they can turn to again and again.

PASSING IT ON

Clearly, album making is a powerful way to build our children's self-esteem and instill in them a feeling of significance and a sense of belonging. Albums also help our kids see and appreciate their strengths, and we can document their lives and their place in the family story.

These are just a few of the benefits your family can enjoy as you preserve your children's past and create a lasting legacy that will forever color and shape their futures. If you reap even one benefit, your time and effort will be well spent. But when it comes to kids and albums, the pages Mom and Dad create are only half the picture. That's because *everybody has a story to tell*— including our children.

Kids can benefit greatly from making their own albums. And in the next chapter, we're going to show you how you can help start them off on the right foot, point them in the right direction, and raise up the next generation of album makers.

Chapter Six

Instilling in Your Child a Love for Story

Train a child in the way he should go,
and when he is old he will not turn from it.
—ANCIENT HEBREW PROVERB

A teacher affects eternity;
he can never tell where his influence stops.
—HENRY ADAMS, *The Education of Henry Adams*

Decades ago, children everywhere loved the tale, *The Counterpane Fairy*. In that magical story, author and illustrator Katharine Pyle's tiny Counterpane Fairy guided children into various adventures by leading them through the squares in a counterpane quilt. As each child looked into an individual square, he or she would fall into that square and into the tale that subsequently unfolded.

Clinical psychologist and neuropsychologist Dr. Enid Reed notes that this story powerfully illustrates the effect of album making on children today. As they look into each quilt square—or album page—they can relive the same wonderful adventures again and again.[1]

Of course, children love to read and listen to stories. But, as every parent knows, they also love to tell stories themselves. Whether they write their own little books or invent an imaginary friend, our children, too, need outlets for their creativity and ways to express their innermost feelings.

Carol Ann Harris told us, "A few weeks before my son turned five, I asked him what he wanted for his birthday. Without missing a beat he said, 'I want my OWN camera and my OWN scrapbook!' Marshall now has his OWN pages in his OWN scrapbook with photos that he took with his OWN camera! And of course his pages include his OWN handwriting. What a treasure!"

MEET TOMORROW'S MEMORY KEEPERS

Today, we are the primary keepers of our family's legacy. But our children and teenagers are the family historians of the future. What we teach them today will remain with them throughout their lives.

And if we start early, what we teach them can be passed on to many others as well. When our kids learn early in life the importance of preserving their memories and stories, they influence their friends, their schools, their families, and future generations. Album making also can build your children's relationships with your family and with their friends—especially those who are making albums of their own.

You may wonder, *But how do I get my kids hooked? I'm just getting started myself!* We assure you that this is not a problem. You two can learn together!

Here are some principles that we have found helpful for parents who are launching their children on the tradition of album making. We're confident that, if you follow these suggestions, you and your child will both achieve great album-making success—and enjoy each other during the process.

- *Lead by example.* The first and most obvious thing we can do to encourage our kids to make albums is to model album making for them. Work on your own personal albums and have your kids sit next to you and learn as you go.
- *Show your interest in making albums together.* Don't just suggest that your child do it on his or her own. Express your interest in spending time together; talk about how much you enjoy making albums with one another.

• *Find out what your child's interests are.* What does your son want to put in an album? Soccer pictures? Stories he's written? Encourage him to include whatever he likes. Make it easy for your children to work on their albums. Give your daughter her own pens and papers, and put

---

(tip)

Album Ideas for Children

Here are a few ideas for theme albums your child might want to try:

1. Sports season (Little League, soccer, and so on)
2. "My Hobbies"
3. "My Friends"
4. First Grade (or Second, or Third, and so on)
5. "My Family"
6. Cheerleading/Dance Team
7. Sweet Sixteen (or any other special birthday)
8. Time Capsule (include a sampling of photos from special events and daily life, as well as memorabilia like receipts for hobbies/ toys, baseball cards, liner notes from a favorite CD, and so on)
9. "A Day in My Life" (include daily activities such as studying, playing video games, getting ready for school, talking on the phone, and so on)
10. Graduation
11. ABC (from "After-School Play Practice" to "Zonked Out After Studying")
12. Favorite professional sports team
13. Celebrities/Heroes (from singer Britney Spears to tennis hero Andre Agassi)
14. Gift (for grandma, a best friend, a coach, or a favorite teacher)
15. "My Dog/Cat"

Your child may already have an idea of what kind of album to create. Use this list to spur ideas as necessary, but encourage your child to think independently and creatively.

them in the dining room or playroom where she has easy access to
them. When there's a time that she doesn't have homework to do and
says she's bored, suggest that the two of you sit down and complete an
album page together.

- *Be helpful.* Sit with your kids and stick with them like photo tape. Get
  them hooked by helping them, but let them do things their own way.
  Give them the freedom to establish their own style. Don't insist that
  they make the pages "perfect" or do them *your* way.

- *Involve others.* Kids understand the importance of friendship, so invite
  your children's friends over to work on albums together. Host a workshop just for kids. Make it a social event, so your kids can see that it's
  fun—not just for moms, but for friends, brothers, sisters, dads, and other
  family members. Meanwhile, practice what you preach: Work on your
  albums with your friends at a time when your children can see you, so
  they can realize how much fun you and your friends have together.

- *Keep them interested.* Children like hands-on activities, and they will
  want to have something to show others after each session. But since
  children's attention spans are relatively short, concentrate on smaller
  projects that take less time. Try shorter theme albums, based on events
  such as the family trip to Disneyland or their recent soccer season.
  Children also do well with ABC albums. Whenever you work with
  kids, include break times.

- *Make a gift album together.* Pool your efforts to make a book for Dad,
  Grandma, Grandpa, or a friend. Give it as a holiday gift, a birthday
  present, or just for fun!

tip

Involve Your Child

When you're making albums with your child, use *we* and *our* a lot, as
in "Doesn't it feel good to be making albums of our family together?"
and "We sure are getting a lot done!" Words like these help kids feel
a sense of ownership of what you are doing together.

- *Keep the albums simple.* Nothing is more intimidating for kids (and new album makers) than the sight of an overly creative album. Remember, just putting pictures in an album counts as being creative! At the same time, allow for individual style.
- *Feed the fun.* To keep your kids going, serve an energy-boosting snack like animal crackers, pretzels, and fruit juice.
- *Get your children started.* Try not to overwhelm them with too many details, but do go over a few basic reasons for making albums and warn them about the dangers of not using photo-safe supplies.

  Encourage kids to
  - select their best photos (kids do well with thematic groupings, such as a friend's surprise party, their own eighth grade graduation, or the regional baseball finals),
  - crop away unwanted parts of their photos,
  - mount their photos (show them how to do this once you've had some practice yourself),
  - journal about what is going on in a photo (have them explain who's in the picture, what was happening at the time, where it took place, when it took place, and why it was fun), and
  - add photo-safe stickers or other memorabilia to jazz up their stories and photos.
- *Give them duplicate photos* or photos for which you have retained the negatives. That way, if important portions of the photos are accidentally cut out, the original is not lost forever.
- *Look for a new twist to your album making in order to motivate yourself and your family to do albums:* Find an unusual or clever element for your pages that can give fresh motivation to do an album project. Rhonda discovered one such motivator by accident:

Rhonda: In 1996, my mom and dad spent the Thanksgiving holiday with us. While they were here, we decided to join together to make an album page for a relative's fifth birthday. As my dad, who is an amateur cartoonist, was sketching one of his classic cartoon people, I got a brilliant idea. "Dad, would you cartoon on an album page—one for each of my kids' books? Do something that reminds you of them and then write one of your little poems to accompany it."

He humbly agreed, and while he was working on the cartoons, I took his picture. I also got shots of three of our kids looking on as Grandpa was creating. Of course they all loved their personalized sketches and funny poems signed, "Love, Grandpa," and I was thrilled with how impressed he was when I reminded him that since he had used a fade-proof pen on acid-free paper, these sketches would be around for hundreds of years. Everyone was happy with the project— the kids, my dad, and especially me!

But another benefit also evolved from that experience. My younger son, Joel, who was thirteen at the time and very reluctant to write or work in albums, decided he would make a photo album of his cartooning sketches and be "like Grandpa." So I provided the album pages, and Joel, who had already been following in my dad's footsteps and developing the skill, started his album with sketches and photos. *Yes!* He started an album on his own, and his enthusiasm inspired the two girls to get out their books as well.

tip

Make It "Child's Choice"

Ask your child what he or she would like to have in an album. Make a list of those preferences: school papers, report cards, drawings, stickers, stories. Then, gather those items and sort them by school year or by month. Narrow your child's choices down to a few items for the first page: three or four photos from a birthday party with one small sheet of stickers, for example. Make sure you have a small, photo-safe album for your child to start with. (Children generally do better with smaller albums because they are less intimidating and easier to complete.) If children are too young to journal on the pages, you can interview them and write down their words. Or children can "journal" by drawing pictures, and you can add explanations in the margins.

• *Give your kids an inexpensive, disposable camera* so that they can take pictures of what's meaningful to them. That way, they have not only their own album to keep, but they have their *own* photos. At first they may take a lot of pictures of caterpillars or baseball mitts. This is especially true of young children. You may want to gently suggest, "You probably don't need twelve pictures of Fuzzy, but one or two would be great!"

No matter how many pictures your children take, they will begin to see what's most important to them. They will be nurtured as they surround themselves with things that give back to them and give them a sense of who they are. When Rhonda was a teenager her mother passed on to Rhonda the responsibility of completing her own albums, saying, "You're old enough to do this yourself now!" Rhonda was able to step forward and start right away because for years she had been closely watching her mother and enjoying their family albums, including ones about her.

One day, your children will be old enough to shoulder the responsibility for their own albums, and the leadership you provide will give them the knowledge and incentive to carry on this tradition. There's no doubt that your child has the creativity that's required. (As we've already said, we all have a natural supply of creativity—and most kids seem to have been given a double dose!) Your children may just need a few words of encouragement, a nudge in the right direction, and an example to follow.

The buck stops with them. But it begins today with you.

PART III

Enriching
Your Present

The now, the here, through which
all future plunges to the past.
—JAMES JOYCE, *Ulysses*

We are tomorrow's past.
—MARY WEBB, *Precious Bane*

Praise they that will Times past, I joy to see
My selfe now live: *this age best pleaseth mee.*
—ROBERT HERRICK, *The Present Time Best Pleaseth*

Chapter Seven

TERRIFIC TRIBUTES

Memory is to love what the saucer is to the cup.
—ELIZABETH BOWEN, *The House in Paris,* 1935

I am certain that after the dust of centuries
has passed over our cities, we, too, will
be remembered not for our victories or defeats
but for our contributions to the human spirit.
—JOHN F. KENNEDY

The *World Book Dictionary* defines recognition as "favorable notice; attention; acceptance...appreciation."[1]; the *Random House Webster's College Dictionary* says that recognition is a "formal acknowledgment conveying approval, sanction, or validity."[2]

We don't know about you, but *we* certainly appreciate getting a little *favorable notice* and *formal acknowledgment* now and then. In fact, we can hardly get enough of it!

MINIMUM DAILY REQUIREMENTS

In today's relatively health-conscious society, millions interested in physical health follow the American Dietetic Association's advice concerning minimum daily dosages of vitamins and minerals. Unfortunately, those of us who might benefit from similar guidance concerning our emotional health are out of luck. To the best of our knowledge, no organization has ever declared an official daily (or weekly or monthly) requirement for recognition or affirmation—though an argument could be made that we need these as much as, if not more than, we need nutritional supplements. Yet even if such a recommendation were ever made, most of us would be hard-pressed to find someone to supply us with that dose.

Think for a moment. When was the last time you went out of your way to make someone feel special? What did you do most recently to show someone that you hold her in high esteem or to tell someone that he's competent, capable, and highly valued? In the last week what have you done to demonstrate to someone—say, your spouse, your child, or your closest friend—that you value and appreciate his or her efforts?

Now, turn the tables. Can you remember the last time someone recognized you or your efforts in an especially positive way? This recognition may have come at work, at home, on a visit with your parents, or during a phone conversation with a friend. How did this interaction make you feel? No doubt you were more than just mildly pleased. You were probably proud of yourself and greatly affirmed in the knowledge that you were appreciated. We'll bet that you were also motivated to do more of whatever got you that recognition in the first place. You probably felt affinity for that encourager as well, a greater sense of loyalty and connection. Perhaps this very minute you are wishing you could get more of that kind of acknowledgment!

Everyone appreciates recognition. Even the least ambitious and unassuming people among us want others to regard them highly. And for good reason. Recognition helps us feel special, which in turn makes us feel valued. When we feel valued, we feel as if we belong. And as we've already pointed out, many top psychologists have emphasized the importance of belonging and significance in a child's life.

In his famous hierarchy of needs, psychologist Abraham Maslow identified love, affection, a sense of belonging, and esteem as being among the most basic human needs. According to Maslow's model, only physiological needs for oxygen, food, water, and safety are more important. And only after these basic needs are met can such "higher" needs as self-actualization, understanding, esthetic appreciation, and spiritual needs be met. Thus, in a very real sense, our albums can play a key role in helping us to become the deepest, richest, and greatest people we can be.

SAY IT WITH PHOTOS AND WORDS

The poet John Donne said, "No man is an island." We cannot agree more. After all, where would any of us be without the parents who lovingly raised us, the former boss who gave us our first "big break," or the grandparents who established our families and held them together through the years? How much poorer our lives would be without the aunts who took us under their wings, the friends who have remained faithful since childhood, and the teachers who insisted we could accomplish anything we set our minds to.

We all have numerous people in our lives for whom we feel grateful. Unfortunately, that gratitude often remains unspoken. Without a specific reason or medium for doing so, most of us fail to express our appreciation to the people we care about most.

One of the best tools we've found for remedying this situation is the tribute album. A tribute album can take many forms and be called by many names: personal album, memory album, or gift album. This type of album can be as short or as long, as simple or as complex as you choose. It can include photos and journaling alone, or it may be packed with letters or memorabilia. You can create a tribute album on your own or with the help of family members, friends, other sports team moms, coworkers, church members, or anyone else you know. But regardless of what the tribute album includes or how it's made, its purpose is to give honor and recognition to a person (or persons) who touched your life.

The year that Linda Elliott's mother, Mary Natali, was headed for her milestone seventy-fifth birthday, Linda and her family decided to create a special album for the occasion, titled: "75 Ways You Have Made a Difference."

Linda compiled a list of her mother's character traits and qualities, ranging from her solid work ethic to her independence and sense of humor. She even included her mother's love for feeding the birds and her love for quilts. Linda had each relative write a letter to Mary (on a ruled album page), telling her what they valued in her and what memories of her they cherished. Under headings like, "You made a difference to David" or "You made a difference to Doug," Linda included these individual letter pages along with photographs of each contributor in the album.

"My mom was overwhelmed by the love we showed," says Linda. "This album is priceless to her. She always keeps it close to her chair, handy to look at and treasure for the rest of her life."

Of course, family members aren't the only ones who deserve tribute albums, as evidenced by this story sent to us by Tracy Meyers and Joyce Corlett.

Mr. Laney, a member of our church for the past thirty-two years and a barber by trade, was moving across the state. Nearly every Sunday of those thirty-two years he served by helping tend to the infants and toddlers in the church's nursery.

So we gave blank album pages with information and ideas to the families of the church, asking that they return their completed two-sided page with written memories, good wishes, and, hopefully, pictures of the children this wonderful man had cared for.

What came back was not only a testimony to his calling, but a history of the church for the past thirty years, depicted through stories and pictures from each family: pictures of the church's 100th anniversary, pictures of many young boys—now in college—getting their first haircuts at Mr. Laney's barbershop, and pictures of children sitting on his lap and at his feet while he enchanted them with a story.

When our pastor presented the album to him, Mr. Laney was speechless. Then he offered thanks for his "wonderful and thoughtful" church family. After the service, he hugged and thanked everyone. Then he walked around sharing his album full of memories.

SHOWING APPRECIATION WITH TRIBUTE ALBUMS

We've found that tribute albums are among the most popular albums people make. This is true for a number of reasons. First, tribute albums provide a unique and lasting way to demonstrate to others how much we love and appreciate them. They create an opportunity to deepen relationships with the person being honored as well as with those doing the honoring. Tribute albums validate the people in our lives who most deserve recognition and appreciation. They celebrate some of the most important relationships in our lives, they allow us to get beyond the superficial, and they're fun to make!

Of course, if we want to give gifts that tell people they are loved, we could easily run to the stationery store and pick up a card. But there's only so much you can do with a card. You sign it, maybe add a little note, and you're done. Or we could write a letter. Letters are always treasured. But because letters generally do not include photographs, they lack the emotional impact of a tribute album. (Remember, "Pictures are worth a thousand words.") Unlike a letter, a tribute album includes both pictures *and* words. In contrast to a card, both the words and the images are created by you, the giver. "The only gift," wrote Ralph Waldo Emerson, "is a portion of thyself."[3] Tribute albums can have a much greater emotional impact than letters. They also are more tangible and often last longer than the spoken word does.

(tip)

Top Ten Tribute Albums

What kind of tribute album would you like to create? Here are ten of the most popular tribute albums we see on a regular basis.

1. Wedding anniversary (golden, silver, and so on)
2. Best friend
3. Coach
4. Teacher (especially for Teacher Appreciation Week)
5. Mother's Day
6. Father's Day
7. Retirement
8. Landmark birthday (forty, fifty, sixty, and so on)
9. Grandparents' Day
10. Best wishes/Farewell (to retirees, coworkers, long-time officers of clubs, and so on)

Imagine that today you receive a phone call from your father. As you listen, he lists eight to ten qualities about you that he especially loves and is proud of. Or maybe the call is from your best friend, who wants you to know just how much your friendship has meant to her over the years.

That call would have a tremendous impact on you. You might walk around grinning for the rest of the day! You'd probably remember your father's or your friend's exact words—for an hour or two, or perhaps for a day. In time, however, the memory would start to fade. You'll recall the phone call itself, but the details of exactly what was said—and *how*—might begin to elude you.

If your father or your friend says those same things in a tribute album, however, those words will be written down, perhaps accompanied by the

---

(tip)

Make It a Group Project

Putting together a tribute album is even easier when you enlist the help of others. Here's a sample letter to help you gather the stories, photographs, and other memorabilia you need:

Dear Friends and Family:

I hope this letter finds you doing well and enjoying the year to its fullest.

I am in the process of creating a gift for _____ and could use your help. The gift is a keepsake photo album filled with letters, stories, and pictures from friends and family. I am enclosing a sheet of photo-safe stationery for you. Please write your memories or a letter on the lined side of the sheet.

Your letter can describe a memorable time you shared or express your best wishes or thanks for the way _____ has influenced your life. If you have a recent photo of yourself or one of the two of you together or with your family, please send that with your letter, and I'll include it in the album. Photos from years ago would be appreciated too. Be sure to explain on a separate visual memory trigger of a photograph or ticket stub, so that you can reread them—and relive the moment—for the rest of your life.

Now, we're not saying that those phone calls aren't important or valuable. And we are definitely *not* saying, "Don't just tell someone good things because they'll only forget your words." Of course not! Every kind and loving word we extend to those around us is powerful and infinitely worthwhile. The words we capture in our albums, however, are powerful and worthwhile as well—and infinitely more lasting. They can go a long way in driving home the beautiful and much-needed message: "You are valuable and truly loved."

Years ago, we read an article in which people were asked, "What is the most meaningful gift you could ever receive?" The number one answer? A

sheet the who, what, when, and where so we can properly place and label the photos (You may want to send reprints because these photos will be used on the album pages and will not be returned.)

I will be presenting this album to _____ on _____. I hope to have the gift completed a few weeks before then. What a thrill it will be for _____ to receive this gift filled with letters and photos from loved ones!

I can't wait to include your memories in this album. Please return your letter and photos to me by _____, so that I have enough time to complete the album. Also, when you mail the package, I suggest you take it directly to the post office so that the correct postage gets affixed.

Thank you so much for your contributions to this album. All the time and effort you put into your letter will mean the world to _____.

Sincerely,

Include a mailing label to make returning the letter and photographs to you even easier.

completed photo album filled with stories, photographs, and letters from loved ones. In short: a tribute album.

Who in your life deserves a tribute?

At one time, the answer to that question for Bill and Sally Wardell was Sally's father, Jerry, who was retiring from the ministry after more than thirty-five years. To complete the album, the family invited forty-five friends and family members to participate. To their surprise, everyone did.

"When the pages came in day after day, Sally and I would pore over them," Bill says. "They were covered with photographs and newspaper clippings. Some pages were journaling only: letters of praise, thanks, and hope. We heard from his fellow pastors, his secretary of many decades, a choir director from Germany, his old friends, and family. We heard from people he served with in Vietnam. People whom he had christened and later married. His sixteen-year-old granddaughter wrote about and drew a picture of the swing he had made her when she visited him as a child.

"Sally and I had the opportunity to read everything before anyone else did. I really got to know my father-in-law better through the many people whose lives he has touched. As a result, I gained a new appreciation for him and his work."

On the day of the celebration, Sally gave Jerry the album. He opened the cover and began turning the pages, seeing the names and faces of people he hadn't seen in years. As he realized what he'd been given, he began to cry.

"The fact that people took photos out of their own collection to both remind him of and thank him for their times together touched Jerry the most," Bill reports. "He said, 'This album is something to be shared, to enjoy, to remember, and to remind me to think back to how long we've all known each other and how much we mean to each other.' "

SAY IT NOW

If you've ever been to a funeral, you probably share our frustration. Whenever either of us attends a gathering after a loved one's death, we find ourselves listening, both touched and perplexed, as family members, friends, coworkers, church members, and others gather to eulogize and say good-bye to the dearly departed. The words they share are tender, moving, touching. What they say is comforting and healing to those who are grieving a loss and celebrating a life. Yet whenever we find ourselves in these situations, we cannot help but think, "If only he or she could hear all the wonderful things being said!" Our loved ones deserve to hear those kind words so that they can appreciate them.

Several years ago, Connie Fintel found herself sifting through thousands of photographs her grandparents had collected over the years. She knew her mother was nearing the end of her life, so, as she sorted, she decided to create a tribute album for her. Connie included photographs that documented every phase of her mother's life from childhood to the present.

"I left large amounts of white space where my mother could write about the pictures and give information I could pass down to my children," she says. "I gave her the album at the beginning of September and asked her to write

A Sentimental Theme

Make an ABC album telling someone twenty-six reasons why you appreciate him or her. Use the ideas in this list—or make up your own!

I'm glad you're my friend because you...

Always are there for me	**N**ever lie
Bring out the best in me	**O**pen your heart
Challenge me	**P**ray for me
Double my fun	**Q**uestion injustice
Excel at loving me	**R**ally behind me
Follow through on your promises	**S**et me free to be me
Give me hugs	**T**ell it like it is
Hold my hand when I need it	**U**nderstand me
Invest time in me	**V**alue good friends
Jest with me	**W**eather the hard times with me
Keep in touch	E**X**ult in my victories
Live a joyful life	**Y**earn for connection with me
Make me laugh	Add **Z**est and **Z**ing to my life!

anything she desired. She returned it at the end of that month. To my surprise, she had written on almost all of the pages, giving not just factual information, but sharing the emotions she had relived as she turned each page."

As it turned out, Connie had created her mother's album just in time. "My mom died a week later, on October 7, but she left me a piece of herself that I can hold forever."

Connie's mother was able to get her stories onto the page quickly because her daughter made it easy for her. First Connie sorted and mounted the photographs. Then she provided enough space for her mother to journal. You, too, can make it easy for others to add to your albums by doing much of the prep work, being clear about what you want them to contribute, and providing the materials they need.

One year, for instance, Rhonda cut up 8½-by-11 pages of acid-free paper into four rectangles and sent the pieces to her relatives

Rhonda: Instead of sending birthday presents or cards to our kids this year, I asked them to send a blessing: a word of encouragement, a prayer, a verse, a note. I said, "Just write something to them on this page."

We got back some of the most beautiful tributes that way! Creating a tribute was easy for each person to do because they only had to make one page—not an entire album. They simply wrote on a plain piece of paper, which I called a "blessing card." I sent smaller sheets, so the task wouldn't be intimidating. (I figured if it looked like too much work, people might not do it.) But some people, like my sister, took two sheets. She put some old photographs with her notes, and all our kids' cousins wrote encouraging notes.

The whole idea was such a hit that we started doing the same thing for our relatives, sending them blessing cards and making album pages. My parents, Mac's parents, and all my siblings have albums, so we just take album pages, add a few photos, and write: "For Father's Day" or "For Your Birthday." Then we add a special tribute or blessing and mail them the whole page.

It feels wonderful to be able to bless somebody. All of us want to love and be loved. A tribute album provides an opportunity to go a giant step beyond saying, "Thanks for the great job you did raising me" or "Thanks for always being there" (though saying those wonderful things is important too). A tribute album creates a big-picture story of our appreciation and love.

Whether you give a completed album or a partially filled album you can add to over the years, tribute pages are a great way of acknowledging and affirming those you love now—before it's too late.

Chapter Eight

CELEBRATING LIFE: SPECIAL EVENTS AND EVERYDAY MOMENTS

To be able to enjoy one's past life is to live twice.
—MARTIAL, *Epigrams*

Bliss in possession will not last;
Remembered joys are never past.
—JAMES MONTGOMERY, "The Little Cloud"

Life is made of moments," writes Anna Quindlen in *A Short Guide to a Happy Life,* "small pieces of glittering mica in a long stretch of gray cement. It would be wonderful if they came to us unsummoned, but particularly in lives as busy as the ones most of us lead now, that won't happen. We have to teach ourselves how to live, really live."[1]

Life is, indeed, composed of shining moments: from high-profile birthdays and anniversaries to low-key, late-afternoon summer sprints through the water sprinkler. In her best-selling gift book, Quindlen beautifully describes the importance of making room in our lives for such priceless experiences.

We agree with her 100 percent. But we would argue that we must not only make *experiencing* these moments a priority; we must also make *capturing* them a priority. Album making not only helps us savor the experience, but it can remind us of how important these memories are to us and motivate us to carve out time for such other experiences. Album making also allows us to, in a sense, do what Quindlen points out cannot traditionally be done: "summon" the moments to experience at will.

CAPTURE THE MEANING BEHIND THE SPECIAL DAYS

The moment your best friend opens the door, you know that all the work— three hours of blowing up balloons and decorating—was worth it. Her eyes shine as your friends jump out from their hiding places, shouting: "Surprise!" And even though the party lasts only half as long as the planning did, the memory will last a lifetime with the help of her album...

Events like graduations, anniversaries, birthdays, holidays, family reunions, showers, parties, baptisms, vacations, award ceremonies, the first day of school, ball tournaments, and more are among the most significant moments in our lives, yet so often we forget the details. We even forget what these events mean to us. That's why in our journaling we need to do more than answer the questions, "Who's in the picture?" "When was it taken?" and "Where was it taken?" As you put together album pages about the special events in your family, ask yourself:

- Why was this day important?
- Why did I take this picture?
- What do I really want to remember?
- What was I feeling at the moment this photo was taken?
- If I could communicate only a handful of details about this day, what would I really want the next generation to know?

Include the answers to these questions—and to questions of your own— on your album pages. Of course, sometimes there isn't much more to say about a photograph than the basics. Occasionally, we may just need to say, "This was the homecoming dance," and leave it at that. But most of the time, there really is more to the story than a single line can tell.

Perhaps every year before their prom, your children and their friends take pictures at each student's house and then go out to eat at a certain special restaurant. Don't forget to write down specific traditions like these! The next generation won't know details like that unless *you* tell them. You might write, "The kids at Central love to go to Atwater's Restaurant every year before the prom. It's one of the most expensive restaurants in town, but dad usually chips in a few bucks. After all, our Jenna is worth it!"

Or you might go a little deeper into your feelings: "This is the last year Evan will be living at home. When we saw him heading out the door to his senior prom, we felt proud and sad at the same time. It's hard to know that our son won't be living under our roof much longer. But we know we couldn't be sending a more wonderful man out into the world."

Proms, graduations, holidays—every special event provides an opportunity to celebrate the days and people you love most. Rhonda's family, for example, has a special tradition:

> **Rhonda**: In our house each family member gets to use a special red
> plate when it's his or her birthday. Many times, I make French toast,
> put a candle in it, and serve it on that plate. We always take a picture
> of the person eating from that plate, which reads: "You're special
> today." By giving our kids that plate to use, we're saying, *You're
> special today—and every day.*

(tip)

A Wedding to Remember

If you are married or planning a wedding, include in your album a copy of your wedding vows, your marriage certificate (original or copy), lyrics from songs or poems performed or read at the ceremony, and receipts showing how much everything cost. (It will be interesting to look back at the prices as time goes by.) Make sure you also include casual photographs taken by family and friends. Or you may have photos your professional photographer took of you getting ready, before and after the ceremony, and so on. Don't use only formal shots. You want to remember the *entire* day.

I always try to write something—either my own thoughts or a meaningful verse or quote—to emphasize the importance of the event. For example, on the page where I've recorded Julia's fourteenth birthday, I wrote a paraphrase of a scripture verse: "I have great confidence in you.… I am greatly encouraged;…my joy knows no bounds."[2] I placed the verse between two photographs of Julia and her sister, Janetta, and then included this caption: "Proud Mother with Lovely Daughters."

Little touches like these help us see past the celebration itself to the significance behind it. When we take photos of our family traditions and celebrations, put them in our albums, and then write about them, we capture the experiences to enjoy again later. We also have an opportunity to write about *how* our children are special. Think about your own family for a moment. What traditions do you have? How did those activities become traditions? What is their significance to you and to your family?

Often, we can enlist the help of our family members to capture each event. This helps give us a slightly different perspective. For Christmas one year, Rhonda's family joined other relatives at her parents' home for dinner. Her mom had to set up a table in their garage in order to accommodate the crowd of twenty. It was ten degrees below zero that day—so it was cold! Rhonda asked her son Jacob to journal about that day in his own album. He wrote: "My favorite thing at Grandma's is to have lefsa and skinny pancakes" and "Grandma served us Christmas dinner in her garage. Of course, Grandma Ada's garage is wallpapered, heated, and has a rug on the floor!"

Jacob's words are simple. But they include important details about specific family customs. They also reflect his obvious fondness for his grandmother. And they reveal some of the things that were most important to him about that day: beloved traditions, great food, and his family. Our words don't have to be eloquent to be meaningful. Like Jacob's, they just have to come from the heart.

One year on Thanksgiving, Lisa Kurzawa wrote her family members' names on diecut paper turkeys and passed them out with gold and silver pens, asking each family member to write down on his or her turkey three things for which they were grateful. Before dinner, they each shared what they wrote.

From Lisa's father, who had recently recovered from a stroke, came this offering: 1) turkey; 2) Thanksgiving Day; and 3) Tony [his caretaker]. Lisa's young son offered up: 1) guys (his name for his favorite action figures); 2) bed ("Wow! He's thankful for going to bed!" Lisa marvels); and 3) home.

Lisa arranged these and the other turkey cutouts on the pages of her album, nestled around photos of her family's Thanksgiving Day celebration. With their help, she can vividly remember for years the first Thanksgiving after her father's stroke. And she is unlikely to forget the pet name of her son's favorite toys even after he is all grown up and married and no longer interested in playing with "guys"!

All too quickly, that fifth birthday or fifteenth anniversary celebration will be over, but the memories can last. Even the tiniest details can be enjoyed over and over again when you preserve them in cherished albums.

SAVOR EVERYDAY MOMENTS

Most of us have grown up with family albums that contain pictures from our birthdays, Fourth of July picnics, and family reunions. But often what's missing

---

tip

Thanks for the Memories

Here are a few ideas to use at Thanksgiving or any other time you want to create a page that reflects your gratitude:

1. Use calendar pages as a gratitude journal. Every day, write down something you're thankful for.
2. Create a "thankfulness album." Mount a photo from each month depicting things or people for whom you are thankful.
3. Use a ruled page to write a letter to your spouse or child. Record all the things about that person for which you are thankful.
4. At a holiday celebration (or just at dinnertime!), set out an album page and ask everyone in the family to write a sentence or two about what they're thankful for.

are photographs of the first day of spring, a great grade on a report card, or the day we learned to tie our shoes. Many of our parents did think to snap a photo of our first solo bike rides. But our albums rarely contain photographs of us as kids riding around the neighborhood streets on an ordinary summer day. Yet these, too, are among the glittering moments in life that we can savor.

What kinds of everyday moments are worth chronicling in our albums? Any and all of them! It might be something as simple as your kids working out an argument by themselves or spending an afternoon in the kitchen making their favorite marshmallow treats. You may snap a photo of your husband working in his office and then journal about how hard he works to provide for the family.

Pages that show such everyday moments provide a balanced view of your family life. One hundred years from now, if someone looked at your album,

---

tip

Time in a Bottle (or an Album)

Imagine how wonderful it would be to have a scrapbook photo album of what it was like to live in the 1900s. Mary Chandler encourages others to create a "Life at the Turn of the Century" album to celebrate life in the new millennium.

To create your own time capsule album, take photos of a few city landmarks, streets, churches, and other local sites to complete a "My City/Town" section. Take pictures of your home, including your kitchen, home entertainment center, computer, and car for the "My Home" section. Other sections can include "My Family," "My Pets," and any other category you choose!

To add details, consult your day planner to help reconstruct recent weeks, months, and even years. All you need to do is transfer the dates you planned ahead for—dentist's appointments, soccer games, and lunches with friends—to blank calendar pages which you can add to your album, and you have an instant time capsule. Your family will have fun poring over this album now as well as decades from now!

could they get an accurate picture of your world? Would they think, *All these people ever did was party?* Or would they see that you also cooked dinner, hoed the garden, held barbecues in the backyard, went to church every Sunday, and helped your children with their homework? Everyday moments include afternoons in the wading pool, eating home-cooked dinners, and making papier-maché volcanoes for the science fair. They include the tablecloth on the table and sitting down at that table as a family. This is how we live our lives. These are the moments worth capturing.

> **Cheryl**: One of the most unflattering photographs of me that exists is one my husband took of me, years ago, when I was mowing the grass. I was sweaty and dirty and wearing an old swimsuit. When he took the photo, I could see him thinking, *Oh, boy. You're going to hate this.* But I can still see that picture so clearly in my mind!
>
> Someday, that will be a fun picture for my kids to have: *Here's Mom, mowing the grass in her swimsuit.* They won't just remember what I looked like when I was dressed up—they'll remember the everyday me. They'll know I was a hard worker. They'll see that I wasn't above getting dirty to get a job done.
>
> There are lots of photos out there of me in my flashy, colorful outfits and big earrings. This photograph balances that image. It tells the rest of the story. When my kids look back on this photo, they'll see me looking grimy and tired…and real. Without pictures like these, my kids would only have part of the story. This way, they can remember all of me.

Sandra Bishop knew that she wanted to document her everyday life, so she decided to take photographs of all the messes her two-year-old, Eli, made in a single day.

On the day she chose, Eli orchestrated about a half a dozen major messes, including completely emptying Sandra's wallet; putting his bath toys in the toilet; flinging magnetic letters off the refrigerator and around the kitchen; and unloading in the entryway a drawer which held binoculars, walkie talkies, a container of pens, and a cupful of pennies. ("That was twenty minutes of my life!" Sandra says.) Sandra also included a photograph of Eli "helping" her clear the table after dinner. "His idea about doing that was actually getting a fork and clearing all the leftover food off the plate and onto the table and floor."

Sandra found herself laughing while taking the photographs. She says, "*That's* what my everyday is like—I bend over a lot, picking up things. Those photographs show the reality of being a parent and the sense of humor required to stay sane."

Sandra made a point of cherishing everyday moments, and we hope you'll do the same. Make sure your album includes Dad reading to the toddlers after work, kids husking just-picked corn on the front porch, the nightly ritual of tucking in a child at night with hug and a prayer, saying grace before each meal or having family devotions, sharing Saturday morning breakfasts with your girl-friends, meeting your child at the bus stop, Grandma canning pickles in the kitchen, and you at your aerobics class. These are the images that will give the next generation the truest sense of your family's traditions, values, and heritage.

Acknowledged and celebrated, these "small" moments can be a source of joy and contentment and, over time, make important statements about who you are and what's important to you.

CELEBRATE YOUR LIFE

We all wear many hats as spouse, parent, child, grandchild, sibling, stay-at-home parent, full- or part-time employee, Sunday-school teacher, community

---

(tip)

Include the Grownups

Cheryl: My daughter is an adult with children of her own. When she looks back on the albums that cover her childhood, she says, "Mom, I wish you would have taken more pictures of the adults." She wants to know what my hair or her dad's looked like when she was growing up. She also wants to know what Uncle Doug looked like. So don't forget to take pictures of the adults as they currently are—and have them tell their stories, too.

volunteer, or business owner. In the busyness of our varied roles, we can too easily lose sight of who we truly are, and that's one reason why we encourage people to create a celebration album. A celebration album is exactly what it sounds like: a celebration of your life. It allows you to step into the spotlight and celebrate your blessings, your achievements, and your everyday moments. Unlike a tribute album, which is about someone else, a celebration album is a statement about *you*. It may include photos, memorabilia, journaling, and other positive reminders of what you value and appreciate, what you've accomplished, and what you aspire to. Between its covers you may find photos of people who care about you, thank-you notes from people you've helped, quotes that make you laugh or think, evidence of the difference you've made in peoples' lives, and reminders of your many blessings.

> **Cheryl**: I once created a celebration album that included two pages
> of my children, two pages of my mother and brothers, two pages of my
> house at the lake, two pages of my dogs, and two pages of my friends.
> I completed my album shortly before I went to Australia on a business
> trip. I knew I would be meeting lots of people, and I thought, *How
> will they know who I am?* So I created this album and called it "Family,
> Friends, and Home."
>
> Once I got to Australia, I passed that book around the room
> whenever I had the opportunity to speak. By the end of the day or the
> talk, the people I was speaking to knew a great deal about me and what
> was important in my life.

Celebration albums can introduce us to others—or they can simply be a gift to ourselves. "My dad wasn't one to compliment me on my efforts or achievements," says Susan Iida-Pederson. "I recall only a few pats on the back from him during my childhood and teen years. So, I was surprised and excited when he wrote an essay about me for a college writing class he was taking. In a one-page reflection, he wrote, 'Susan is someone who has always met life head-on and prevailed; a levelheaded, social person with a sense of humor and welcome flair for writing, what any parent would like to see in his offspring. I am, indeed, fortunate and proud.'

"I carried that essay in my purse for years after I received it, reading and rereading every line. I am always uplifted by its precious and humbling words. But I couldn't carry it around in my purse forever, and it's not the sort of thing one displays on a refrigerator or wall. So, what could I do with this important piece of writing? How could I keep its message intact and accessible?

"*I know!* I thought. *A celebration album!* (Must be what dad meant by 'level-headed'—that uncanny ability to figure out these things.) My dad's essay would be the centerpiece.

Celebrate Every Day

Every moment of your life is worth celebrating. Melanie Leach's album includes such moments as

- a child holding flowers from the backyard for mom
- blowing bubbles in the backyard
- going to the dentist
- playing dress up
- having chicken pox
- playing in the backyard tree house and creek
- finding creatures in the yard like frogs and turtles
- going to the grocery store
- playing with favorite toys
- Dad at work
- being outside and inside of the church
- playing at Grandma and Grandpa's house (a weekly event)

What everyday moments would you most like to capture? Make a list of eight to ten. Then put a fresh roll of film in your camera if it's empty and watch for those moments this week. As soon as you get the photos developed, make a point of adding them to your album pages and journaling about them, so that in months or years to come you won't think, *Now what did I take these photos for?* There won't be any question because you'll have those stories down on paper!

"When I first thought of doing a celebration album, I wasn't sure what to include or whether I had enough positive stuff to fill an eight-by-ten album. But finding a photo here, a card there, a few meaningful quotes and stories, I began to consider an even larger book to hold all I had to celebrate. On the title page of my album, which reads in large, capital letters: "ME," I set a very clear expectation: "This album is about me, by me, and for me—it is, quite frankly and without apology, an album that celebrates who I am!"

Below, in her own words, Susan describes some pages from her album. Let them trigger ideas for your own album.

- "A page of beautiful black-and-white childhood photos taken by my dad, a professional photographer, reminds me to be grateful for a happy, healthy childhood."

- "Photos of my peaceful home on the banks of the Mississippi River remind me to be grateful for my surroundings, for nature, and for a place that's become a haven from the world's madness."

- "Pictures of my husband, family, and friends remind me to be grateful for all the love and support we give each other."

- "A couple of pages of cards and letters from people impacted by something I wrote or said remind me to be grateful for a job I'm impassioned about and for work that helps me make a difference."

- "A page titled Rituals and Celebrations includes photos and/or words that remind me to be grateful for the small, everyday pleasures like chopping and stacking wood, fishing with my husband, reading by the fire, good music, and good chocolate."

- "A collage of photos of people laughing—that hold-your-sides, face-stretching kind of laughter—reminds me to be grateful for the fun and joy in my life. It also reminds me to stop taking myself so seriously."

- "The final page in my album says it all and reminds me to be positive and appreciative. It is a photo of color balloons, along with a quote from Tim Hansel's *Holy Sweat,* which I found in *A Place Called Simplicity:* 'Until further notice...Celebrate Everything!' "[3]

Celebration albums will be more than an affirmation of who you are. They are also a way for you to communicate who you are to future generations. What do you want your kids and grandkids to know about you and to remember about you? These are the wonderful details of which celebration albums are made.

FROM SPECIAL DAYS TO EVERY DAY

Whether it's Saint Patrick's Day or pizza night, every day is an occasion worth commemorating. As you decide what to put in your albums, we hope you'll make a point of including big and small events—just as the world brings big and small events into your life.

From the "glittering mica" to the "gray cement," each moment is worth remembering, cherishing, and celebrating. Each one is an irreplaceable gift worth treasuring for a lifetime.

Chapter Nine

DREAMING BIG DREAMS

We are the music makers,
We are the dreamers of dreams…
—ARTHUR O'SHAUGHNESSY, *Ode*

We are such stuff
As dreams are made on…
—WILLIAM SHAKESPEARE, *The Tempest*

In her *New York Times* number one bestseller *Life Makeovers,* personal coach Cheryl Richardson asks the hard-hitting question, "How often do you day-dream about living a better life—a life that reflects more of *you,* your values and deepest desires?" She goes on to make a statement that should surprise none of us who live in American society, where people are always looking for some new key to satisfaction: "In today's world most people live with a nag-ging sense that something's missing or that life is passing them by."[1]

Do you ever long for something more? Do you ache over the unfulfilled dreams of your youth? Do you have a vision of what you'd like to accomplish tomorrow and twenty years from now? If so, are you taking steps today to reach those dreams? And if not, why not? What is getting in your way?

Many of us recoil from the subject of dreams. We scold ourselves for being greedy. *I should be content with what I have,* we think. Or, worse, we get hung up on what we've lost in the past, telling ourselves, *There's no point in dreaming dreams that will never come true.*

It is impossible to make it through life without experiencing failure and disappointment. For some of us, those setbacks have been mere speed bumps on the road of life. But for countless others, dreaming is something that is relegated to the past. We see it as something for which we don't have the time or the energy. The few dreams that do manage to survive are hustled to the corners of our minds like difficult children: *Wait over here until I can deal with you.*

We like to think that we will revisit our dreams once we have time. *After the kids are in all in grade school…* we think, or *After the last one is away at college, I'll dream.* We imagine that we'll be able to start dreaming and working toward fulfilling those dreams once we get that elusive promotion or after we retire.

It is tempting to think of dreaming and pursuing dreams as a luxury that costs more time, energy, and even hope than we can afford. Yet we easily ignore the much greater cost that the abandonment of our dreams takes on our spirits.

The toll on our practical, everyday lives is also great. In a study conducted by Harvard University, researchers tracked the accomplishments of 1953 MBA graduates. Of those surveyed, 70 percent claimed that they valued goal setting, yet only 3 percent had written plans for achieving their goals. Two decades later, in 1985, the 3 percent who had written out their goals were worth more financially than the other 97 percent combined.[2]

While financial success is not the most important, nor the only, goal we can pursue, this research illustrates the powerful effects of writing down our dreams. Whether we are reaching for financial success or seeking to fulfill the desires of our hearts, we simply cannot afford *not* to get our hopes and goals onto the pages of our albums.

GETTING THOSE GOALS ON PAPER

Beth Lambdin was raised in a family that believed in dreams. Her mother especially believed firmly in the importance of having life dreams and goals. "From my earliest remembrance," Beth says, "I can remember her saying,

'Let's make a list of all the things you want to do in your lifetime.' " As a result of her mother's prompting, Beth has kept such a list almost her entire life. But five years ago, she took her list of dreams to a new level.

At that time, Beth got the idea of combining her list of dreams with her love for making albums. She chose a single album in which to record her dreams. She began with one dream, which she wrote down on the top of a page. Then she moved on to the second dream and a second page. Over the next three years, she kept adding dreams to her book—one per page. Beth now has seventy-two dreams in her album. "And I add to it on a regular basis!" she says.

Today, eight of Beth's dreams have been realized—and sixty-four are simply waiting to be fulfilled. Most of the dreams represent big events that one day will be documented in her family albums, where she puts most of her pic-

---

tip

Dream Big and Wide

Your dreams will likely be quite diverse, but you may also see some themes develop. Consider using the following topics as the focus of one page, several pages, or an entire album (or albums):

1. Love
2. Friends (monthly game parties, getaway weekends, and so on)
3. Career goals
4. Accomplishments (a mix of acts of kindness, grades in school, weight loss, promotions at work, and so on)
5. Travel
6. Family (adoptions, activities with children, weekly breakfasts with Mom, and so on)
7. Hobbies
8. "Recipes I Want to Try" (or other things you want to learn)
9. Sports accomplishments (reaching different levels in karate, improving your golf game, and so on)
10. Acts of kindness (random or planned, anonymous or identified)

tures. But the dream album will always have at least one or two photographs to show how a dream became a reality.

The dreams, says Beth, can be serious or silly. Hers range from "Get a mud bath" to "Write a book." She's even included "Take dance lessons with my husband."

"I figure if I put that one in there, he'll have to do it if someday it's the only one left that's not fulfilled!" she laughs.

The dreams that Beth has seen fulfilled include significant ones, such as, with her husband, starting a private Christian high school in her area; smaller goals, like making a tribute album for her mother (a project to which Beth's brother and sisters also contributed); and midsized goals, like hiring a part-time personal assistant to help her in her work.

On the page about her personal assistant, Beth included a photograph of Rachel Ruiz and journaled about the experience of hiring her. On every dream page, Beth answers the question, *How did this actually happen?* "I always write about how the dream came to pass."

Beth's dream album nurtures and encourages her in a variety of ways. It gives her a sense of accomplishment by reminding her of what she's already done. It provides a record of the blessings in her life. It also helps her set priorities and creates a sense of urgency. Beth says, "I always wanted to make an album for my mom. But I'm not sure we would have gotten to it if I hadn't included that goal in an album and then asked as I looked through it, 'Okay, what can I accomplish this year that's in this book?' " Beth has also found that other people love looking at her album and that it inspires them, too, to start dreaming.

Of course, the goal in keeping a dream album is to realize as many of our dreams as possible—all of them, if we can. But occasionally, dreams do not come true. Beth advises, "If someday you find that a dream cannot be fulfilled, the best way to fill that page is by journaling your thoughts and feelings about that dream's not coming to reality and looking for the lessons you learned along the way." But don't give up too soon! Dreams that you hope will come true this year may yet be fulfilled!

Getting our dreams down on paper helps open the door to achieving them in more ways than one. Seeing evidence that some dreams have come

Find Your Dreams

As time passes, many of us lose sight of our dreams. Here are a few ways to reconnect with your former hopes and goals:

- *Ask "What if?"* Do you ever think, *What would have happened if I had finished getting my degree?* or *I wonder if I could have been good at art if I had ever really tried.* Spend a few moments taking stock of your answers. The point is not to question the choices you have made or to second-guess where you are today, but to discover clues about how you can further enrich your life.

- *Remove roadblocks.* Make a list of obstacles that are keeping you from realizing your dreams. It may be money, or perhaps it is a lack of belief that you can actually accomplish what you desire. Take a moment to imagine that these barriers no longer exist. Allow yourself to enjoy a rich sense of possibility. Repeat this exercise each day for a week and let the feelings it evokes fuel your dreams.

- *Set a date.* Choose a date by which you want to achieve at least one of your goals. Place a reminder in your day planner or calendar two weeks and one week before this date. Plan a reward that you will give yourself if you complete it.

- *Picture yourself succeeding.* Create for your album a colorful collage using images from magazines that represents the fulfillment of your dreams. If you want to get a promotion at work, you might select an image of a person who looks successful in a given field. If you long to start a family, you might use pictures of children. If you dream of taking home a softball trophy, find an image of athletes sliding into home base.

- *One step at a time.* Break each of your goals into manageable, doable steps. You can do this with all your goals or start with three to five. Don't forget to document in your album each success, no matter how big or small!

true, for instance, helps inspire confidence that other dreams can become a reality as well. Sharing our albums with others also creates opportunities that otherwise would not have occurred. For example, one of Beth's dreams is to "See the birth of a baby." Since sharing that album with friends, she has had a number of offers from people who have invited her to watch their child being born. The best part, however, according to Beth, is the impact album making has had on her five daughters. "You know how kids are. They do exactly what Mom does!"

Beth's eleven-year-old daughter, Michelle, has started a dream album of her own. Beth says it's a blessing "to watch her be so purposeful about her life and really think about the things she wants to see come to pass."

One of the dreams that Michelle put in her album last year was that she wanted to go to the presidential inauguration in January. "Michelle has always loved politics," her mother says. "Another of her 'adult' dreams is to run for office someday."

So Michelle asked if she could volunteer for the Republican Central Committee as part of a homeschool project in the fall of 2000. She worked in the office every Tuesday and got very involved in the election. She then decided that if George Bush won, she wanted to go to Washington to watch the swearing in ceremony.

Michelle raised the money for airfare, obtained tickets from her congressman, and invited her two, fourteen-year-old cousins and an adult friend of the family to join her. Numerous newspapers interviewed Michelle, and she included all those articles in her dream album.

"I know it would not have happened if she had not taken the time to think about what she wants to do in her life," Beth says. "Putting her ideas down in writing helped compel her to actually accomplish her dream."

What are a few dreams that you would put on your list? Get a master's degree? Earn a black belt? Act in a play? Our friend Shari MacDonald created a dream album for herself (which includes "Adopt a child from another country" and "Go to Venice with Craig") and gave another to her husband to fill with his own goals ("Chop down a tree" and "Buy a brand new Porsche 911 Turbo!").

On a page in her album, Kresha Waldrop wrote down her resolutions for the new year, including "I will learn to quilt," "I will send love letters to my husband," and "I will keep my photo albums up-to-date."

All dreams are worthwhile, and each one represents values and desires that are important to you. So start your list today. You'll find that it's fun—and liberating—to start dreaming.

You may even be surprised at how quickly your dreams start coming true.

PART IV

Inspiring Hope for Your Future

Memory is not so brilliant as hope,
but it is more beautiful,
and a thousand times as true.
—GEORGE DENNISON PRENTICE, *Prenticeana*

What would the future of man be
if it were devoid of memory?
—ELIE WIESEL, *From the Kingdom of Memory*

What a strange thing is memory, and hope;
one looks backward, the other forward;
one is of today, the other of tomorrow.
—GRANDMA MOSES, *My Life's History*

Chapter Ten

PASSING ON
LIFE'S LESSONS

Those who do not remember the past
are condemned to repeat it.
—GEORGE SANTAYANA

Wisdom is the principal thing;
therefore get wisdom:
and with all thy getting get understanding.
—ANCIENT HEBREW PROVERB

As a young woman living in Amsterdam in the 1930s, Etty Hillesum kept a journal that chronicled her life before and during her imprisonment in a Nazi concentration camp. In her diaries, Hillesum wrote, "There is nothing else for it, I shall have to solve my own problems. I always get the feeling that when I solve them for myself I shall have solved them for a thousand other women."[1] Hillesum recognized that learning does not remain in a vacuum. As we learn, we pass on our newly acquired wisdom to others.

When we create our albums, we learn a lot. We work through the experiences of our lives, and we learn about our roots, ourselves, and many other things as we go. And the "thousand others" who read our pages—our friends, our children, our children's children—will learn from our stories as well.

Life is full of lessons just waiting to be learned. For example, in recent years we've learned that, although our loved ones care for us, they cannot always be there when we need them. We've also found that blessings come to us time and again, independent of what we've done and regardless of how much we do or don't deserve them. We've seen that good people often suffer and that scoundrels sometimes succeed, and that, somehow, we survive—and even thrive—in spite of it all. We've also discovered that, no matter how many lessons life brings, another always follows closely on the heels of the last.

Your experience has probably been the same. And when you capture these lessons on the pages of your albums, you and your children can both benefit, as you personally seek to avoid hardship in the future and as you attempt to pass wisdom on to your kids.

Some of the lessons we memory keepers (and our loved ones) learn through our albums, we learn almost by accident. As we are flipping through the pages, we suddenly develop a deeper understanding of how blessed, or how loved, we are. Or we realize that we are working too much or not seeing our friends or family as much as we'd like. If we are open, this insight can be a catalyst for personal growth and change.

Other lessons about a specific subject we are interested in—or simply about life—can be learned as we purposefully attempt to come to a greater understanding of ourselves and the world in which we live.

If you love quilting, for example, you might keep an album that's filled with both photographs of your work and of the ribbons you've won at quilt shows. You might also include bits of information you learn about quilting, notes from your conversations with other quilt makers, and insights and metaphors about life you discover through your work.

Or, you might choose to create an album that focuses on women or men who have had a particularly powerful impact on your life. Each page might include one or more paragraphs, along with reflections about what each person means to you and what you have learned from each one of them.

The approach you take is up to you. As with the entire process of album making, anything goes! What matters most is that you take advantage of this opportunity for you—and your children—to learn and grow.

GETTING YOUR LIFE LESSONS INTO ALBUMS

As you've undoubtedly concluded, you can do many things with your life lessons. You might include these personal insights in your family album, or perhaps in a celebration album, or you could create a special "Lessons I've Learned" album just for this purpose.

If you like the idea of using your albums to store the wisdom that comes with living, try asking yourself on a daily or weekly basis, "What lessons am I learning?" and "What recent events have had an impact on me?" Write your answers down someplace where you can refer back to them later. From time to time transfer these insights into your albums, so that the lessons you've learned can inspire you and those you love. Practicing this habit faithfully will bring you a sense of great fulfillment.

Susan Iida-Pederson offers this example: "One day a few years ago, I was scrambling to get our place ready for weekend company, and my husband had to remind me to be more aware of what's really important about our home and surroundings. I wanted to capture this truth he'd reminded me of, and I struggled for some time to put it in words. Finally, when I realized I didn't have to write an English 101 theme and could just highlight some thoughts with bullets and phrases, I knew what I had to do."

The page Susan created that day included the following:

In Minnesota—Land of 10,000 Lakes—the phrase
"At the Lake" has special meaning.

- It's an end-of-the-week, casual, barefoot kind of time.
- It's no phones, calendars, clocks, or planned events.
- It's early sunrise fishing or late sleep-ins and dinner at dark.
- It's wet towels and swimsuits on the clothesline, tracking sand across the linoleum floor, and wearing the same jeans all weekend long.
- It's a time of casualness, comfortableness, and community.

There's no more powerful way to communicate the reasons behind our actions than through words and pictures. It's not necessary to create a special Life Lessons album—although, as we said earlier, that is certainly an option. The reality is that lessons are a part of life—and our albums are about our lives. Each of our small stories can be integrated into the greater story of our life.

Susan's page would have fit perfectly into many different albums, including a celebration album or a family album. The type of album did not matter; what she wrote on the page *did.* Because she took the time to put her thoughts down on paper, she was able to discover what mattered most to her about her home. She learned that her frantic efforts to please others and her concerns about neatness and order were in conflict with her reasons for loving her lakeside home: It was a place of refuge that provided "a time of casualness, comfortableness, and community." Once Susan recognized these inconsistencies, she was able to reevaluate her situation and redirect her energies in a way that allowed her to enjoy her home once again.

Other life lessons come to us in more structured, traditional ways. Christiane M. Belisle wrote to us about how her son's interest in World War II catapulted the two of them on an unforgettable journey of discovery and learning that led them to a greater appreciation for and pride in their ancestry.

"I was born in Eastern France after World War II, and I grew up hearing wartime stories," Christiane says. "I had seen every movie made about D-Day, but in the summer of 1998 our family saw the movie *Saving Private Ryan.* All of us were emotionally touched by the story, particularly my oldest son, Marc, who was twenty-four. He began reading about that period in history, and he wanted to visit the Normandy beaches. He reflected a lot on the fact that he might never have been born were it not for D-Day and the Allied Forces. (I am French; my husband, American. We met at a U.S. Air Force base in England.)

"In March of 1999, I came across a bargain fare to Paris, and Marc and I flew over and drove all over Normandy and Brittany, visiting many of the beaches, the Peace Museum in Caen, the Airborne Museum at Sainte-Mère-Eglise, and Omaha Beach Cemetery. My son, a journalist at our local paper, wrote a powerful editorial about what he'd learned:

Through all of my history studies in college and high school, I never understood how much the events of World War II affected the world in which I live.… We, who live securely in an America buffered by two giant oceans, do not realize that our lives were profoundly affected by the sacrifices made by Americans and the other Allied nations during World War II.[2]

"Of course I took pictures of our trip," says Christiane, "so I collected all of our photographs and made an eight-by-ten album for Marc as a Christmas present. I included excerpts of both Stephen Ambrose's *D-Day* and General Eisenhower's order the morning of the invasion. I tried to capture the moment in those few pages and to really make it meaningful by including details about certain individuals, such as the first British soldier killed and the first American killed.

"The last item in the scrapbook is my son's article for the paper. We're both very proud of this album. It has a lot of sentimental value, and it displays the history that is part of our Franco-American heritage."

As Christiane would affirm, life offers a wide range of learning opportunities. That's one reason why, for several years now, Rhonda has been using her albums to record the life lessons that she's experienced. She keeps a spiral notebook beside her bed, and several times a week she asks herself what she's learning. Then she writes down the thoughts and insights that come to her.

Rhonda: I try to write in my notebook several times a week. I don't write long entries (I do longer ones on the computer), but I do try to write consistently. Sometimes I write about something I've just learned, or I write about how a Bible verse I just read has applied specifically to my life that day.

Because I still want a long-lasting record of what I'm learning, however, I've started transferring the most important lessons from the spiral notebook into a photo album, with an appropriate picture whenever I have one.

For example, I recently came to the realization that I had to change the way I was doing my job. At the time, I was flying a lot, and I was feeling a lot of stress related to the traveling.

One night, I wound up sleeping in the bathroom of the airport in Lansing, Michigan, because of a missed flight. I realized then that I was not being fair to my family or my work. I was trying to juggle too many things and keep everyone happy—both at Creative Memories and in my family. Exhausted mentally and physically, I had reached the end of my rope. (Sure enough, just weeks later I was diagnosed with the painful chronic sinus and ear block I previously mentioned.)

In my notebook I wrote about what I was feeling. Later, I transferred my thoughts into my album along with a photo that represented my work. I used a photo of Cheryl and me from our latest Creative Memories catalog since I didn't have a photograph of me from the airport in Lansing (which is probably a good thing!). This page reminds me that I can only do so much—and that I have to take care of myself.

Life lessons can come from any experience and any person. You may learn from your coworkers, your boss, your spouse, your children, your parents, or your friends. Or lessons can come to you from books, teaching tapes, movies, or sermons—just about anywhere! As much as you can, keep an eye out for these lessons and write them down so you can transfer them into your albums.

TEACHING THE NEXT GENERATION

It is likely that no one is more ready to learn than our children. It is also entirely possible that our photo albums can be very effective instructional tools.

Albums Teach Our Children Perseverance

Our children's albums and our family albums provide a fun, natural medium through which to communicate important truths to our children. For example, we can communicate a powerful message to a child who is struggling to ride his bike by documenting his progress in our album pages. If riding his first two-wheeler comes easily to your son, you may write something like, "I rode on my own my very first try!" If he falters, however, you can still include the "learning to ride a bike" story in the album. Only this time the message might be: "I try hard—and I keep on trying!" You might add a photograph of your husband as a boy, along with a story about how he practiced for three weeks with training wheels before he ultimately succeeded. You can include an account of how determined and faithful your child was as he continued to learn how to keep his balance.

Through your album pages, you can communicate to your child both that

Create an Affirmation Album

When Lea Kelly was discussing the power of journaling, an acquaintance offered the following story:

"This woman told me that when her youngest daughter was fourteen, they went through some really tough relational stuff," Lea said. "So she decided to start a journal and every day write at least one good thing that she noticed her daughter had done. She also told her daughter about it and said that the journal would be out on the coffee table for her to read.

"At first it was difficult to think of things to write because their relationship was so strained. She wrote things like, 'You cleared off the table.' But as she began to be more observant of her daughter, she found more things to write about—and both she and her daughter began to change. After two weeks, their relationship was mending, and her daughter said, 'I didn't think you noticed, Mom. Now, I know you do.' "

Start a journal to help you record positive thoughts and observations about your child. Then create an Affirmation Album to bring your words alive with photos. You might include calendar pages, recording in each box one wonderful thing your child or spouse did that had an impact on you that day. On the opposite page, mount four to six of your favorite photos of that family member, ideally from that same month. Add some pages every month.

he is not expected to ride the bike on his own the very first day and that you have complete faith that he will succeed in riding on his own at exactly the right time. By handling our children's stories and experiences carefully, we can help them look at their "failures" in a way that teaches optimism and perseverance. Even more importantly, we can teach our children realistic expectations about themselves and life in general.

Albums Teach Our Children About Developing Character

Melanie Leach created an album she called "What Is a Man?" to help teach her oldest son, Caleb, those traits which she and her husband hope he will develop as he grows. One portion of this album was specifically designed to reinforce Caleb's relationship with his younger brother, Aidan. Melanie included a simple poem, entitled "Example," next to a photograph of the two boys climbing on a log:

Examples

He dreams of being you, you know,
Of running faster and knowing more.
He dreams of being you.
His small feet fly to catch up to yours, to be right
  by your side.
Content to play the sidekick to your superhero role,
He builds you up and drives you nuts because he
  dreams of being you.
He wants to try to ride your bike or wear your shoes
  to play,
He's a follower and a tagalong,
A little brother, close behind.
As I write this, Caleb, you are five and Aidan is two.
While content to play by himself, he looks forward to
  picking you up from school, saying, "I hope my
  dude had a good day."
You have had your disagreements, but you really are friends.

Aidan does dream of being like you, wanting to keep up
But often held back by his size or shyness.
At times, you don't notice him, caught up in your
    pretending games or older friends.
Other times, you turn back to generously encourage him.
This book is called "What Is a Man?"
Your dad and I pray that, with God's help, we will be
    able to share with you the answers to that question.
Yet you have someone to answer to as well.
You are Aidan's best daily example of how to grow into
    a godly man, and believe me,
He watches you very closely.
You can choose to ignore him as a pesky little brother,
Or you can encourage him as a best friend.
He dreams of being like you.
You can make that a dream of being kind, compas-
    sionate, and courageous.
That is the true meaning of being a big brother.[3]

"My son is six," Melanie says, "so, obviously, he can't yet understand the depth of this album's meaning. But the fact that my sons continually ask to look at their albums and have me read those things over and over again to them lets me know that the albums *are* speaking to their hearts."

Damon and Lea Kelly decided to create character albums for their two sons, Taylor and Trent. Each boy has his own ABC album that focuses on one letter and character quality per page. Each page also features a picture of that child, living out that particular character quality. For example, the second page of Taylor's album reads: "B is for Brave" and features a photograph of him getting into the ocean for the first time—something he did even though he was feeling fearful.

The albums, says Lea, provide their sons with "a yardstick to measure character qualities they can see. They can say, 'Here's a time when I really put *this* into practice' or 'I want to see more of *this* in my life.' It's also a way we can say to them, 'These are the things that we value and that we're praying about for you. We want you to be a caring boy, valiant and zealous.' "

Albums Teach Our Children about Values

We also can influence our children's values through our own stories recorded in the pages of the family album. For example, as we document the events of our everyday lives, we may show the church picnics, family reunions, and dance recitals that show our faith, love of family, and appreciation of the arts. Or we may choose to take photographs of particular events in our lives in order to teach about the things we want our children to care about, such as driving the Meals on Wheels route (caring for the sick and the elderly) or participating in a beach cleanup (protecting the environment).

Do Your Heart Good

Missy Rice created what she calls an "album of virtues" for her children, which depicts her family members doing good deeds. This type of album teaches the importance of caring for others, celebrates the best in humanity, and provides a place for many miscellaneous, leftover photos! Examples from Missy's book include photos of her toddler sharing his ball with another baby and her husband working hard at putting their swing set together.

Missy suggests using one of two approaches to making an album of virtues: You can first list the values you'd like to highlight and then find photos which best illustrate each value, or you can let your photos suggest which virtues to include. Here are just a few examples:

- Sharing—children playing together, a child sharing an ice cream cone with a dog
- Love—family hugging, children kissing, dog and cat snuggling
- Respect—children with grandparents
- Gentleness—children with pets or flowers
- Cleanliness—bath time photos
- Determination—sports team members or coach, hiking photos
- Faithfulness—great-grandparents on their fiftieth anniversary
- Joy—a party, someone laughing
- Courage—child taking swim lessons, sports team photos

As your child looks through your albums, she may think, *Here's Mom, sorting clothes at the Salvation Army. I'm going to do that someday!* or *There's Dad, mowing Grandma's neighbor's lawn. If Dad can do that, maybe I can, too.*

Albums Drive Home Life's Tough Lessons for Our Children

Photo albums can also be used to drive home some of the harder lessons in life. Few of us instinctively think of a tough learning experience as something we want to celebrate in our albums. But hard knocks are great learning opportunities for our kids (and for us), and that makes them important events to remember and review!

> **Rhonda**: Last year, one of my daughters got in trouble at school and was fined $50. We felt that it was important for her to earn that money and pay the fine herself, so she had to get a job.
>
> The first day she left for work, we took a picture of her, all dressed up in her uniform. She also wrote a letter to us, apologizing for the deed she got in trouble for. I reduced that letter on a copy machine and put it on an album page, along with the photograph. At the top of the page, I wrote: "Self-Control." Together, Janetta and I wrote about how she is developing the inner strength that will help her say no to peer pressure in the future.

Handled sensitively, stories like this can be among the most important— and, ultimately, the most appreciated and influential—in our children's albums. Our children will draw upon these lessons throughout their lifetime. And just think of how grateful our grandchildren will be to learn that their parents— and we, their grandparents—messed up sometimes, too!

Albums Teach Our Children How to Handle New Situations

We can use our albums to help our children understand new situations they face in life. A six year old who is heading off to school for the first time may find comfort in sitting down with her mom to look through her older brother's "First Day of School" pages. Or a child who is afraid of dogs may benefit from looking at photographs and hearing stories about beloved mutts from the family's history.

Sonja Flockhart used a baby book she'd created for her oldest son to help him understand the family's newest arrival.

I recently gave birth to another son. Our first son, Andrew, was very excited about the baby—until he realized that the baby was going to stay with us. I decided to spend some quality time alone with Andrew, so we sat down and looked through his baby album. It was a very special time for us as I explained that he was once a baby too and showed him pictures of himself as a baby.

He was especially excited about the pictures of Mom and Dad and grandparents holding Baby Andrew. I think he understood that babies need to be held a lot and that they can't do much except cry. I was really glad that I had a baby album for him to see. He loves to look through it and see himself, and it was a special bonding time for us with a new baby around.

THE SKY'S THE LIMIT

As you've probably guessed by now, there is no limit either to the kinds of stories you can use in your albums or to the ways life lessons can be taught through them. Perseverance, inner strength, forgiveness, self-confidence, patience, honesty, teamwork, faith—lessons about these virtues and countless other issues may find their way into your pages.

Regardless of what lessons your albums hold, you can be sure that they are helping to instill emotional and spiritual health in both you and your children—and that, by commemorating these stories in your albums, you are ensuring they are not lost, and will be remembered by you and your family for decades to come.

You'll also find reason to hope that no struggle is wasted. Like the Holocaust survivor, Etty Hillesum, you, too, can help a "thousand others" through the problems you face and the victories you achieve.

Chapter Eleven

HEALING LIFE'S HURTS

What beastly incidents our memories
insist on cherishing!…the ugly and disgusting.…
The beautiful things we have
to keep diaries to remember!
—EUGENE O'NEILL, *Strange Interlude*

What wound did ever heal
but by degrees?
—WILLIAM SHAKESPEARE, *Othello*

In the 1994 film *Shadowlands,* Oxford don and author C. S. "Jack" Lewis, played by Anthony Hopkins, finds himself wrestling on a personal level with a question he has lectured on overconfidently throughout his academic career: Does our suffering mean anything?

Faced with the greatest struggle of his adult life, Jack—who has acted as a sort of advocate of pain—ironically attempts to postpone dealing with his anguish. At this moment, a brash, honest, and cherished loved one challenges him to face his darker emotions by insisting: "The pain then is part of the happiness now."[1]

JOY AND PAIN: AN UNEASY PARTNERSHIP

Like Hopkins's Lewis, most of us are at least tempted to avoid or deny negative emotions like anger, hurt, loneliness, and grief. For one thing, these emotions simply are unpleasant to go through. For another, it's often difficult at the time to sense or remember that they can have a positive influence in our lives. But just as imminent pain is a part of present joy, past and future hope are inextricably linked to our times of heartache.

You might be thinking, *What?! Are you telling me that I should document the pain and suffering in my life? Whatever for? I didn't enjoy going through those experiences the first time, so why on earth would I choose to relive them? Besides, aren't scrapbooks supposed to be fun to read? Why would anyone want to read about my pain?*

The answers to these questions don't come easily. Yet, in our talks to album makers across the country, we have become more and more convinced that including hard events and painful situations in our albums can be therapeutic. Facing the pain of the past can bring about tremendous healing.

Most of us realize that pain is an unavoidable part of our stories. "Who," wrote Aeschylus in *Agamemnon,* "except the gods, / can live time through forever without any pain?"[2] So, if we want to have an accurate record of our lives, we can't skip the chronicling of at least some difficulty.

Yet pain's inevitability does not seem reason enough to choose to record it. Rather, the purpose of documenting our suffering and hardship may be to help us identify and remember the often surprising gifts such experiences bring. C. S. Lewis argued that it is through our suffering that we are perfected, proclaiming, "Pain insists upon being attended to. God whispers to us in our pleasures, speaks in our conscience, but shouts in our pain: it is His megaphone to rouse a deaf world."[3] Sophocles theorized in *Electra,* "There is no success without hardship."[4] On a more sentimental note, Wordsworth suggested that we are "more able to endure, / As more exposed to suffering and distress; / Thence, also, more alive to tenderness."[5]

Clearly, philosophers and artists have long been proclaiming the virtues of suffering and hardship. Yet if we are to reap the ultimate benefits of pain in our lives, we must choose to remember that pain. The words and photographs in our albums can play a key role in our healing, helping us find strength and hope when, in other difficult times, we feel that we cannot go on. This encouragement comes in countless ways. Our albums, for instance, can heal our perspective on the past, provide a nontraditional outlet for our grief, support us in times of physical healing, help us establish family ties, and show us the hope that grows out of our pain.

Albums Heal Our Perspective on the Past

Heidi Everett had always felt embarrassed about her parents' divorce, which happened when she was a young child. Heidi felt, of course, the pain that children naturally experience when their parents end their marriage. But Heidi also keenly felt the loss of her family history. As is common, the messiness of divorce had caused the sharing of family stories to become quite complicated. As a result, Heidi knew little about her childhood. Lost were details about everything from how she was raised to how her distant relatives lived. Once she started raising her own sons, Branden and Brody, Heidi decided that she would learn about her past.

Several years earlier, while helping her mother move into a new house, Heidi had come across a container of old photographs that she had never seen before. In 1997, she called her mother and asked her to bring the photographs to her house so that she could get them into albums.

Her mother put Heidi off until Thanksgiving of 1998, so Heidi gave her an ultimatum: "I'm not letting you in the house unless you bring those photographs!"

At that time, Heidi was in the practice of hosting holiday get-togethers, and she invited both her parents and their spouses. "My rationale was that they'd been divorced for twenty-five years and should be able to tolerate each other," Heidi reasoned. That year, after dinner, she and her mother sat down at the dining room table to sort through the pictures.

Heidi learned all kinds of details about her family. She learned that her Grandpa Axtell had driven a Greyhound bus. She learned that her great uncles had lived on the same farm in Michigan from 1912 to 1980—and that they never had running water or electricity! (But they *had* buried jars of money around the property.)

Soon, everyone was gathered around the dining room table, grabbing pictures, remembering stories from their childhoods, and laughing until the tears came. At one point, Heidi's father picked up a photograph of her mother,

Facing Hard Times

Albums can help us work through some of the hardest times in our lives. Here are a few difficulties they can help us process:
- parents' divorce
- personal divorce or separation
- death of a child, a family member, or friend
- miscarriage
- major surgery
- strained relationship with a teen (or other friend or relative)
- house fire
- flood or other natural disaster
- broken/lost relationship (such as family estrangement)

Make a list of the three most difficult experiences from the last ten years of your life. Then pick the one that you'd most like to work through in an album.

Next, sort through your photographs and find images from that time period. Jot down stories and details you'd like to write about. Decide whether you want to incorporate these into your family album or whether you want to create an album expressly to remember and learn from your difficult time.

Make the commitment to begin one page this week. Allow yourself all the time you need to complete it. Remember that, while you *do* want to get your albums done, sometimes the process of creating the album can be just as valuable as having the final product. So don't rush yourself—and don't push yourself to do anything you're not yet emotionally ready to do. Allow this process to help you work through your pain and find a sense of healing and closure.

taken when she was pregnant with one of their boys, and said, "Y'know, Alice Mae, you certainly were a hot number." She smiled and said, "Well, thanks, DeWain. We have great kids."

That was the first compliment Heidi could remember either one of her parents paying the other. Hearing it brought her a great sense of healing. Sorting through her family's memories and history also helped Heidi gain an appreciation for the way she was raised.

"Yes, my folks divorced," she says. "Yes, we had some really hard times financially and emotionally. But, as a result of this upbringing, I gained independence. I learned how to survive under difficult situations.

"Since that Thanksgiving, I've learned that my history is my history. It made me who I am today, and I am proud of who I am. And I am proud of the lessons that I can pass on to my children."

Albums Help Us Process Our Grief

Whenever we experience tremendous loss, we enter into a period of both tremendous grief and tremendous potential for growth. Album making provides a healthy way for us to enter into mourning and process our feelings of grief.

In March of 1998, Brandi Diamond's daughter Delaney was stillborn. Brandi and her family were devastated. But, she says, "I worked very hard on my grief, facing it as best I could. One way I survived the ordeal was to create an album of the few memories and items I had. It was very healing for me to touch the items and tell my story; I couldn't leave out such an important event in our lives."

In her album, Brandi reported such important details as the location of Delaney's memorial brick and the resting place of her remains. She also included sympathy cards that she and her husband had received, as well as a hospital printout of Delaney's ultrasound. Other families who have lost infants, Brandi says, have included keepsakes given to them by the hospital, such as a lock of their baby's hair or footprints or handprints. They might put in photographs, if they have them and they are appropriate to share, or a letter that they've written to their baby.

Two years after Delaney's death, Brandi found herself working on her son

Taylor's baby album. This time, the experience was pure joy. Yet Brandi remains so convinced of the value of album making for processing grief that she and her friend Brenda Eller lead a grief class for other mothers who have lost babies and want to remember them in this special way.

"Most people do grieving in traditional ways," says Brandi. "This is something that's more cathartic. It releases them to make their child's life real again." The loss of a child in the womb or shortly after birth can be particularly tragic—and confusing. "You try so hard to forget," says Brandi. "But you're also afraid that you won't remember. My album allows me a place to go back and remember."

It also allows her to connect with others about her child's life. "It gives people a place to look. They say, 'Gosh, this isn't something she just talked about. There really was a baby, and here are pictures to prove it and stories and cards from people who loved them.' "

Brandi chose to create an album specifically dedicated to her daughter; others, like Sandra Bishop, choose to integrate into the family album stories about the child they've lost.

After Sandra's daughter was stillborn at twenty weeks, Sandra carefully documented the details of Haley's life and death.

"I am glad I put her story in my album," she says. "It's placed between my husband Glenn's birthday and Mother's Day. For a long time I was hesitant to include it, because I thought, *Oh, it's going to embarrass people or make people uncomfortable,* but death and loss are part of life. In terms of our friends and family, it would be easy just to avoid the subject. But I see people pausing when they look at those pages, and it helps us reconnect to a very significant part of our lives. Glenn and I bonded really deeply over Haley's death. The album pages are a reminder to me that we can grow through life's difficult times and that there's purpose in pain."

All too often we think of album making as an activity that is enjoyed by women. Yet men, too, are finding tremendous solace in this nontraditional tool for processing grief.

For years, Lee Crum's wife, Kristi, had been urging him to create an album of his own. Then Lee's father was diagnosed with cancer. Before his father's death, Lee took him on a fishing trip to Alaska. "I knew when I left that I would take the time to do that album when I got back," Lee says, "because that trip would be something that I would remember forever. So I was meticulous with my picture taking, and I took a journal with me. At the end of every day before I went to bed, I journaled everything we did on that day. When I got home, I sat down with the pictures I had taken, got my journal out, and began to relive the trip on the pages of the album. My dad passed away a year later. Today, this album is one of the few ways that his memory continues to live, especially for my kids. They probably look at that album a couple times a month, just to see him."

Lee did not spend a lot of time or energy on designs or embellishments. His album doesn't contain stickers or decoration. It just simply and beautifully chronicles the story of one of the most important times of his life.

Because Lee was so careful in his journaling, the album includes lots of fun details about the trip. Next to a picture of his father, an avid photographer, taking a shot of the Portage Glacier, Lee wrote: "Both of us being raised in south Texas, it was very unusual for us to see icebergs floating in water." Tiny details like these make Lee's memories real when he reads those pages today.

"My dad is alive to me in that album," Lee says. "Making that album was a very special way for me to have embodied his memory."

At some point in our lives (hopefully later, rather than sooner), all of us will lose our parents and other loved ones. At such crucial times, albums—perhaps more than any other tangible object—can help us find our way through the pain.

Albums Support Us Through Our Physical Healing

For centuries, physicians, philosophers, and religious leaders have asserted that physical healing is impacted by the attitude of the one afflicted. One ancient proverb says: "A cheerful heart is good medicine, but a crushed spirit dries up the bones."[6]

More recently, statistics have linked success in physical healing from injury and disease to positive attitudes in patients. Our albums can be extremely useful tools for fostering attitudes that contribute to greater health. Each of us has experienced this firsthand.

Cheryl: The reality of this connection between attitude and healing was demonstrated powerfully in my own life in the early 1990s after I was diagnosed with breast cancer. In the months that followed my diagnosis, I processed my numerous emotions and found myself turning again and again to album making for comfort.

One of my favorite albums that I created during this time was one packed with cards. At the time of my illness, I had recently celebrated a milestone birthday (that's as specific as I'll get!), and I still had the stacks of cards that I had received during that celebration. I also had piles of other cards that I had been saving for nearly fifteen years. My collection included birthday cards, Christmas cards, and—once chemotherapy started—get well cards.

During the difficult weeks of my treatment, I sat on my bed at night and sorted those cards by size. Doing this was very important to me. I didn't keep every card; I did not use many that were merely signed, for example. But I kept those that were especially funny or touching, the ones that included little notes, personal touches, or photographs, and I put them all in my special book.

Working on my albums was extremely comforting and very thera-peutic, particularly because at the time of my illness many people who were close to me began to pull away. Some probably didn't know what to say to me. Others might have been afraid that I would die and were attempting to detach emotionally in order to minimize their own suf-fering. Regardless of their reasons, their behavior was difficult and confusing for me.

So whenever I started feeling lonely or abandoned, I would open my book of cards to see tangible evidence of how loved I am! As I looked at the pages and pages filled with cards, I easily saw that, over the years, many wonderful people have cared about me. That made all the difference in the world—for me personally and, many doctors would argue, for my recovery. In the midst of everything I was facing, working on my albums is one of the primary things that got me through.

Albums Help Heal Relationships

Another key benefit of albums is that they can help bring hurting people together by fostering communication. In this book, we've already discussed many ways albums can unite people—particularly family members. Nowhere is that reuniting more poignant than in the healing of broken relationships.

Our albums can also foster communication with those with whom we have been estranged. Kathleen Hart tells the story of her friend Debi, who reported that her albums had gotten her through a long weekend visit with her in-laws. Her husband's parents had visited after a long period of being somewhat estranged from them.

tip

A Positive Go-Between for Loved Ones

What do you want to tell your loved ones through your albums? What types of albums or album pages can you create to help facilitate greater communication? Write down in an abbreviated version three messages you want your child (or spouse) to hear. For example, "We expect an awful lot from Elizabeth. Sometimes we may push too hard because we know she's brilliant. We're so proud of her! We want to do everything we can to help her succeed. We just need to remember to let her be a kid, too!"

So start your own journal and let your loved one know where to find it. Make sure you include only affirmation and positive communication in this book. (Disagreements can be handled in some other forum.) Add to your journal regularly—and regularly add those entries to your albums (either your family albums or albums created just for this purpose), where they can be enjoyed and shared.

During their time together, Debi brought out the three albums she had completed over the past year: one for each of her children (ages eighteen, sixteen, and ten). Through these albums, Debi's in-laws were able to catch up on the time they had missed. That morning, they pored over the pages. Then, after a short lunch break, they went right back to the albums! Most of the photos depicted events that the grandparents had not been a part of, and many told stories that they were seeing and hearing for the first time. But because they were able to immerse themselves in the stories captured in the albums, they were able to feel very much a part of their grandchildren's lives again. The result? Debi's albums helped her and her in-laws get past an awkward moment—and helped a hurting family begin to communicate again.

Albums Reveal the Hope in the Pain

With time, good is often found in even the harshest of life's circumstances. Chronicling our experiences clearly and honestly can help us find that good.

We all know that life is filled with many struggles and heartaches, but at times life brings us more than we think we can possibly bear. In 1999, Tanya Klein and her family suffered a series of tragedies comparable only to the trials of the biblical character Job.

To help her in her healing, Tanya chronicled the events in a special album. "I needed to create this album for me more than for anyone else," she wrote to her children. "This album represents hours and hours of sleepless nights, tears, rereading and rewriting. It represents my heart and all that was in it. Never in my life had I gone through such agony and torment. I had to get my words down on paper so that in the future, hopefully, all your questions about this period in our family's life would be answered."

In August of 1999, Tanya and her family lost her husband Tim's mother, Vivian, to cancer just ten days after the Kleins' son, Ryan, underwent surgery to remove his tonsils and adenoids (a surgery that was later determined to have been unnecessary). The family was grieving deeply. Vivian had deteriorated quickly, and the emotional stress of losing her so suddenly was taking its toll on everyone. Tim in particular was suffering. "It was an awful time. Many tears, much sorrow and sadness," Tanya journaled.

Nine days after they buried Vivian, Tim left town to help settle his mother's affairs. That morning, Tanya and their children, Ryan and Morgan, spent time in the family's basement office. Then they left for church to see Tanya's sister get baptized. Before they left, Tanya noticed a slight burning smell that was indicative of the trouble they'd been having with their computer, and she turned it off. When Tanya returned home after lunch, she opened the door to an overwhelming cloud of smoke.

> You could normally see right into the kitchen, but I couldn't see anything but black. I unlocked the door and pushed it open. The thick, black, toxic-smelling smoke caught me by surprise as it bellowed out of the door and into my face and mouth. I choked on it so badly that I fell on the deck coughing. I couldn't catch my breath. In between coughs I was screaming for [our cat] Ariel to please come out! She didn't.
>
> I got up off the deck and ran next door to our neighbor's house so they could call 911. I ran back to the house, and I collapsed on the ground in the grass screaming, "Oh God, no! Not this! Not now! We can't go through this right now. Tim just can't handle it!"

Reaching for an outlet for her emotions, Tanya opened her heart and spilled her feelings out onto the page. She included devastating details:

> We lost 95 percent of everything due to the smoke damage or the fire itself. The smell of smoke is horrible. I can't describe it…

Tanya's album is brimming with honest questions and emotions: *Why did this happen? Could I have done something differently?* Yet it is also laced with hope. "My healing process came one sentence and one tear at a time," Tanya says today. "With each tear came one more memory to journal, each one taking me one step closer to God." And Tanya will never forget what she learned through the process:

> As I end this story that I have worked on for more than three months, understand that it is all about heart. Tim and I will never view life as we did before. Once you have suffered spiritual brokenness, you don't

want to go back. As bad as it has been, no one can "fix" us. We don't want to be fixed. We view life differently now. We take life one day at a time, and we pray that, whatever hurdle is around the next corner for us, we will be able to handle it spiritually.

It is our prayer that you never suffer a tragedy like Tanya's. But we do know that, like us, you will face great hardships as well as tremendous joys in this life. As you deal with the unique challenges—both large and small—that your life brings, may you, too, find hope and healing in the album pages of your touching, amazing, one-of-a-kind life story.

Chapter Twelve

SIGNS OF
THE MIRACULOUS

Spirit is an invisible force made visible in all life.
—MAYA ANGELOU,
Wouldn't Take Nothing for My Journey Now

The heavens declare the glory of God;
the skies proclaim the work of his hands.
—ANCIENT HEBREW PSALM

Evangelist Oral Roberts was famous for telling people to "Expect a miracle."[1] Author Jean Cocteau stated, "Picasso said that everything is a miracle, that it's a miracle that we don't dissolve in our baths."[2] And Thoreau argued that people often focus on ancient, biblical miracles "because there is no miracle in their lives. Cease to gnaw that crust. There is ripe fruit over your head."[3]

Our theory is this: Evidence of miracles is constantly being added to your photo albums or being left out of your photo albums. The question is not whether miracles occur, but whether we recognize them and what we do with them.

Each one of us experiences turning points in our lives. Far more often than we realize, these turning points are what many would call miraculous. Unfortunately, most of us fail to recognize the miraculous in our lives because we don't know what to look for. We think that experiencing the miraculous means finding a long-lost brother living down our block or surviving an earthquake in India. We imagine, *If I inherited a castle in Scotland or discovered a cure for cancer,* then *I would have a miraculous story to tell!* But incredible events are occurring all the time. When we capture our life experiences in albums, we are more able to recognize this, and this awareness causes us to look at our lives with new eyes.

Sometimes, of course, we don't see the miraculous because we either don't expect to or we don't want to. But once we acknowledge the presence of miracles, we can begin to see signs of them everywhere!

Think back to the last time you bought a car. If you purchased a silver Volkswagen, you probably began to see silver Volkswagens all over the road. It's a common phenomenon. The same principle applies to spotting miracles. Once you recognize that miracles are real and that they happen to *you,* you begin to find them around every corner.

FINDING MIRACLES IN THE ORDINARY

Of course, some of us may need a little push before we begin to recognize the miraculous.

> **Rhonda**: In our twenty-one years of marriage, my husband and I have witnessed numerous miracles in our lives. We now believe that they occur every day, but I couldn't see them at first. Then something happened that convinced me that the miraculous is all around us.
>
> The following experience taught me two key lessons: First, don't just look at outward appearances. I need to let faith move me beyond what my human eyes can see into experiencing the miraculous. Second, be diligent about looking for and recording the miraculous events that occur around me every day.
>
> Ever since Mac was a teenager, he'd wanted to adopt a child in desperate need. He'd communicated this passion to me even before we were married and, with love-struck compliance, I had mumbled my support. But I forgot about it even more quickly than I had agreed to it.

Three months after the birth of our second son, however, my devotion was put to the test when Mac said to me, "Now that we have two biological children, I feel the time has come to reconfirm our decision to adopt."

Adopt? That word cut like a knife. I reacted with sadness and anger. After all, I was still physically capable of bearing children. Not only that, but the health risks of needy children were great. We didn't have the money for lots of medical bills. Besides, it was my right to bear children! Mac couldn't deny me that...could he?

Yet Mac's conviction stayed strong, and he lovingly persisted. The time came for me to make a decision. Did I have faith or not? After hours of tears, I made the decision to believe for the miraculous, whatever that meant.

The first miracle that occurred was the transformation of my heart. By the time we had completed the long and complicated adoption process, I was an excited, "expectant" mother, anxious to hear about our new child.

Two beautiful miracles followed—Janetta and, later, Julia. Miraculously, both girls thrived physically. Miraculously, we bonded with them just as we had with our biological sons. Miraculously, we've always had the money we needed to take care of all of our children. Miraculously, our lives have turned out richer and fuller than anything I ever could have dreamed of or orchestrated.

I will always be thankful for this challenging experience because it got my eyes off outward appearances and bolstered my wavering belief in the miraculous. I am also thankful that I have the story documented in detail in our albums where it continues to strengthen my faith and feed my spirit every day.

CHRONICLING THE MIRACULOUS

Author Os Hillman claims that God "allows each of us to experience trials, testings, miracles, and challenges in life that are designed to provide 'faith experiences.'"[4] Edith Schaefer calls these turning points or spiritual markers "signposts."[5] Even those of us who do not consider ourselves religious can recognize the presence of the miraculous and the significance of such signposts in our lives.

Signposts may be answers to prayer or simply miraculous provision or direction that arrives at those times in life when we need it most. A signpost might be an unexpected check in the exact amount needed to pay the electric bill; an acceptance letter from a school we long to attend; a fortuitous job promotion; or a reluctant, but ultimately profitable, move to a distant state. With each signpost, we may sense at the time— or recognize later—what appears to be the hand of a greater force working behind the scenes. Whether because of our faith or independent of any faith, we sense that we have been gently nudged along a path that leads to our ultimate good.

Despite our protests to the contrary, we all have miraculous stories to tell. Perhaps your date for the prom got sick and couldn't go, so his older brother stepped in—and now you and "big brother" are about to celebrate your fifteenth wedding anniversary. Or after the infertility tests were confirmed, you and your husband decided to adopt a baby from China. Your passion for adoption grew, and now you're the editor for an international adoption magazine.

The truth is that our daily lives are brimming with signposts that miraculously direct us. For those of us who value the development of our spirits, formally or informally, the strengthening of our faith can be one of the greatest rewards of chronicling the miraculous.

In recent years, Rhonda has been so influenced by evidence of the miraculous in her life that she has begun to focus more and more on a process she calls "faithbooking." Faithbooking is the process of chronicling life's signposts in order to encourage us in our daily lives. There are two primary approaches to faithbooking: 1) incorporating faithbook pages into all our albums; and 2) creating faithbooks dedicated specifically to the miraculous.

For many years, Rhonda has woven stories of faith into her everyday photo albums. For example, several pages tell the story of how seemingly divinely-orchestrated events made it possible for her and her family to purchase a piece of property in St. Cloud where they had long dreamed of building their home.

tip

Count Your Blessings

In the film *America's Sweethearts,* movie star Eddie Thomas (John Cusak) embraces thankfulness as a tool to help him get over a broken relationship. "I'm grateful for the sun," he says, looking for the good in his life. "I'm grateful for the moon."

As he sets out to face a particularly challenging situation, Eddie is given an important piece of advice by his spiritual mentor: "Don't forget to be grateful."

What inspires gratitude in your heart? Your mother's potato salad? The smooth ivory of piano keys? Your spouse? Your kids? The scent of freshly cut grass?

Begin a list today. Keep it in your wallet, in your checkbook, or on your refrigerator. We've heard of people writing their list on a big sheet of butcher paper that is posted on the wall. Wherever you keep your list, commit to the practice of adding to it daily.

From the greatest things ("My son's birth") to the tiniest ("Finding an unexpected stash of Halloween candy in July"), this list of blessings can help you feel rich, loved, and more appreciative than you have in years.

Here's a brief list to get you started:
- the first star at night
- wet dog kisses
- the smell of a baby's head
- unexpected compliments
- strong teeth
- being cancer free (a big one if you've ever had cancer—as well as if you have not)
- dew on spider webs
- a promotion at work
- the glow of fireflies
- chance meetings (with a friend at a bookstore or with a new love)

What's on *your* list of blessings?

Naomi Shedd, on the other hand, tends to make albums specifically devoted to the topic of faith and miracles. In one of her faithbooks, which she calls "God's Fingerprints," Naomi includes blank calendar pages which she has filled in with the days of the month and details of the miraculous events that have occurred on different days. For example, on January 5, Naomi wrote, "God heals Ruth of cancer." On the opposite side of the page, she included a photograph of her friend Ruth on a skiing trip—a vacation which Ruth took at a time when she would have been undergoing surgery. A smaller miracle recorded on the same page is the time Naomi felt called to a particular location to look for—and find—a lost receipt. All levels of miracles, she says, help build her faith.

These approaches to faithbooking are distinctive, but both have the same goal: to capture the miraculous stories in our lives. You cannot choose wrong as long as you get your stories down in the pages of your albums!

Faithbooks serve a number of purposes. They can

- document the signposts in your life.
- teach and reinforce family values and beliefs.
- instruct you like a sacred text or a book of proverbs or fables can.
- extol the characteristics and deeds of the heroes and mentors in your lives who have given you inspiration, courage, and hope.

What are some of the significant signposts you've experienced in your life? Make a list of eight to ten events. Consider how you can incorporate these stories into your albums. Would you like to create a book dedicated solely to these stories? Can you use these stories as anchors for your family albums, spending extra time journaling your thoughts and feelings about these particular experiences? Are there any objects you can photograph or draw that represent the miracle of what happened? Do you have old journals or day planners with old notes about any of those events? As you document these events in your album, you will be surprised at how your eyes are opened to other signs of the miraculous.

Even before you actually start putting together your pages, begin sharing all those stories with your spouse (if you haven't done so before) and with your children. It's amazing how many stories we *think* our kids know that they don't!

ALBUMS AS LIVING HOPE

When our albums remind us of the miraculous events in our lives, they bring us great encouragement, especially at those times when we most need a boost of confidence.

Rhonda: One such miraculous event occurred a number of years ago. While I was attending a Creative Memories Regional Convention, my husband, Mac, flew to Madras, India, to escort my assistant Marcy Miller's newly adopted twenty-one-month-old daughter, Jana, home.

Mac had never been an escort before, nor had he been to India. He had to bring his own first-aid kit in case he got hurt, and he was given sixty pounds of medical supplies—donated to the orphanage's medical unit by a pediatrician from Michigan. Those could have targeted Mac as a potential drug dealer. I have not seen him that nervous since June 1981, when I went into labor with our first child. (He actually fainted then.)

Mac mustered all his courage and made it to India, where he spent a week. There were many challenges in India, but the trip home had even more.

Mac and Jana's flight took them from Madras to New Delhi, to Amsterdam, and then on to Minneapolis via Toronto. In Toronto, they had less than an hour to get through customs. Five minutes before his flight, Mac realized they were not going to make it. He felt so disappointed for Marcy and her husband, Jeff, knowing that they would be anxiously waiting for their baby in Minneapolis. Mac and Jana had come so far. Their trip had already been more than thirty hours long, and they had overcome so many other obstacles. To be this close and miss the flight! Mac knew that there was nothing he could do except pray that somehow they would be able to get on that plane.

They finally made it through customs and proceeded to the gate. Much to Mac's surprise, the plane was still sitting there. The airline agent said, "Well, sir, you are very fortunate. The plane should have left twenty minutes ago, but too much fuel was added and the law requires us to burn off the excess. We will go ahead and let you board." You can imagine how excited Mac was when the flight attendants extended the Jetway and let them on the plane!

That story is documented in our albums and provides us with at least two important lessons. First, it gives our four children an example of a real-life hero—their dad. Second, it's a reminder that miraculous things do happen even when the outward circumstances look bleak.

Do you ever have those days when you feel as if your hopes and dreams have flown away? Do you sometimes feel overwhelmed by how the circumstances and situations around you look? At times like these, you need to pick up your photo albums and remind yourselves of the miraculous. Find hope as you remember situations that seemed impossible, yet turned out well. Your albums can be sources of living hope.

As you continue to work on your photo albums, our wish is that you will take the time to write down the stories and events that are happening in your life so that you have this living hope to go back to time and time again. Record the amazing stories; write about your heroes and the miracles that are shaping your life right now. You'll reap the benefits of your efforts today and for years to come.

An Attitude of Gratitude

Buy an inexpensive calendar this week and write "Things I'm Thankful For" at the top next to the month and year. Make a commitment to jot down something each day, whether it's big ("June 24: Buyers accepted our bid on the house!") or small ("October 16: Found my favorite sour apple/caramel candy at the drugstore today"). When the month is over, add your calendar page to your album. Decorate the opposite page with photographs related to your blessings.

Leave your calendar by your bed and make sure you write down one item for each day.

Robin Scharding shared with us the story of her friend Annette Piper, who told Robin she wanted to create an eightieth birthday album for her mother, Violet. Annette quietly gathered photos, birthday wishes, and stories from approximately fifty friends and relatives. The album was completed, and this special gift was given at a large gathering of friends and family.

The album was a great success. Everyone enjoyed seeing their own contribution on display (including the youngest ones in the family who had submitted crayon drawings). Violet called Annette a week later and said, "I'm so glad you put those plastic sleeves on the pages. I have cried so many tears over the album, surely it would have been ruined."

The album clearly touched Violet's heart, but it brought another significant and unexpected result. At that time, Annette's Uncle Bob had been suffering from Alzheimer's disease. A once-vibrant man whose education included a Ph.D. in nuclear physics, Bob had not spoken nor shown any emotion in six months.

But when he and his wife visited Violet, he started looking at the album. He began to smile. His wife asked what he was doing and he said, "I am reading." Then he began to read out loud a story about his wife.

The family members cherish that moment. It was the first they had heard Uncle Bob's voice or seen his emotions in a long time. By that point in his illness, they all had begun to wonder if he understood things, remembered them, or felt any emotions at all anymore. They now have their answer.

The world is thick with miracles like these.

Which ones will you remember?

CONCLUSION

Learn from yesterday, live for today,
hope for tomorrow.

—ANONYMOUS

Everyone has a story to tell.

We hope that by now you believe it. More than that, we hope you're ready to do something about it.

Back in 1987, when we first started talking about teaching people how to preserve their stories in safe, meaningful photo albums, our dream was that one day everyone would have shelves of albums that contain the stories and pictures of their lives. This dream has yet to be fulfilled, but we are getting closer every day.

Each day, more and more people are catching the vision for creating a legacy through keepsake albums. All around the world, people are preserving their photographs "the Creative Memories way." Perhaps, like them, you have already begun to use keepsake albums to nurture your family, honor your heritage, and celebrate life. Or you may be poised now to begin.

What are your long-term dreams for your album making? Do you want to build your child's self-esteem? Preserve the memories of your courtship and marriage for future generations? Establish a sense of family history and a feeling of connection? Leave a lasting legacy for future generations? Create a page-turning history of the miracles in your life? Whatever your desire, your efforts to that end will bring you great joy and many small victories. Your albums will be created and your legacy built one page at a time. The results will make a big difference in the lives of those you love: your spouse, your children, your extended family, your friends.

We hope we have inspired you to make working on your albums a priority. It doesn't take much to get started. Try reserving one weekend every three or four months to do nothing but work on your albums. Host a workshop. Pair up with an album-making friend twice a month. Or schedule a special weekly time to work by yourself. As in the case of the tortoise and the hare, slow and steady wins the race. But every step—swift or halting—will get you closer to what you want: beautiful, treasured, completed albums.

Picture your great-great-grandchildren looking at a photo album about you. What will they be able to say? What legacy will you leave? The answer will be determined by the decisions you make today. So seize the day! If you really want to make albums, you'll find a way.

In fact, each new day is an opportunity. Decide right now what steps you want to take to make an album legacy become a reality. Set long-term goals. Write them down so you'll be prepared to do the daily activities that will bring you closer and closer to fulfilling your dreams.

You're in this for the long haul, and you are going to make a real difference. Album making isn't just a hobby. It's the creation of a legacy.

You are an album maker—for life!

Notes

Introduction

1. Beth Burkstrand, "Scrapbook Mania: Pricey Labor of Love," *Wall Street Journal* (New York), 16 July 1997, Eastern edition, sec. B, 1:3.

2. Cliff Annicelli, "Memories in the Making," *Playthings*, November 1997, 45.

3. Annicelli, "Memories," 43, 45.

Chapter One

1. Alexandra Johnson, *Leaving a Trace: The Art of Transforming a Life into Stories* (Boston, New York, London: Little, Brown and Company, 2001), 1-3.

2. Johnson, *Leaving a Trace*, 4.

3. Arthur K. Robertson and William Proctor, *Work a 4-Hour Day* (New York: Avon, 1994), i.

4. Robertson and Proctor, *4-Hour Day*, 4.

Chapter Two

1. *Satellite Sisters*, introduction to the Satellite Sisters radio program. Used by permission.

2. Gerard Manley Hopkins, "As Kingfishers Catch Fire," *Gerard Manley Hopkins (The Oxford Authors)* (Oxford: Oxford University Press, 1986), 129.

3. *Gratefulness Bulletin*, series 2, no. 7. Used with permission by Character Training Institute, http://www.characterfirst.com.

Chapter Three

1. *Hope Floats*, Twentieth Century Fox Home Entertainment, 1998.

2. *Moulin Rouge*, Bazmark Entertainment, 2001.

3. Sheila Bender, *Keeping a Journal You Love* (Cincinnati: Walking Stick Press, 2001), 11.

4. Sarah Bailey, "This Year's Lovers," *Elle*, U.K. edition, August 2001, 60.

Chapter Four

1. Dr. James C. Dobson from *God's Protection During War and Peace*, Focus on the Family © 1993, 2000. All rights reserved. Used by permission of James C. Dobson.

2. Faith Popcorn, *Clicking: 17 Trends that Drive Your Business and Your Life* (New York: HarperCollins, 1996), 126.

3. Statistics taken from http://www.faithpopcorn.com.

4. Popcorn, *Clicking*, 126.

Chapter Five

1. Dorothy Law Nolte, Ph.D., and Rachel Harris, *Children Learn What They Live: Parenting to Inspire Values* (New York: Workman, 1998), vi-vii. Poem, "Children Learn What They Live," copyright © 1972 by Dorothy Law Nolte.

2. Proverbs 25:25.

3. Stevanne Auerbach, Ph.D., *Dr. Toy's Smart Play: How to Raise a Child with a High PQ* *Play Quotient* (New York: St. Martin's, 1998), 222.

4. From an April 28, 2001, interview with Dr. Stevanne Auerbach.

5. From an April 28, 2001, interview with Dr. Stevanne Auerbach.

6. Dr. Benjamin Spock, *Dr. Spock's Baby and Child Care* (New York: Pocket Books, 1945), 426-7.

7. Statistics taken from http://www.aacap.org/publications/factsfam/suicide.htm.

8. Tom McMahon, "It Works for Us," *The Oregonian*, 1 September 1999, E03.

Chapter Six

1. From a May 1, 2001, interview with Dr. Enid Reed.

Chapter Seven

1. Clarence L. Barnhart and Robert K. Barnhart, ed., *World Book Dictionary,* vol. 2, L–Z (Chicago: World Book, A Scott Fetzer Company, 1989), 1744.

2. *Random House Webster's College Dictionary* (New York: Random House, 1991), 1126.

3. Ralph Waldo Emerson, "Gifts," *Essays: Second Series* (Boston and New York: Houghton Mifflin, 1876), 161.

Chapter Eight

1. Anna Quindlen, *A Short Guide to a Happy Life* (New York: Random House, 2000), 41-2.

2. 2 Corinthians 7:4.

3. Time Hansel, *Holy Sweat* (Waco, Tex.: Word, 1987), 143, as quoted by Claire Cloninger, *A Place Called Simplicity* (Eugene, Oreg.: Harvest House, 1993), 157.

Chapter Nine

1. Cheryl Richardson, *Life Makeovers* (New York: Broadway, 2000), 1.

2. Bill Phillips, *Body for Life* (New York: HarperCollins, 1999), 26.

Chapter Ten

1. Etty Hillesum, *An Interrupted Life: The Diaries of Etty Hillesum 1941-43* (New York: Washington Square, 1981), 35.

2. Marc Belisle, "French Beaches Serve As a Reminder," 28 March 1999, *The Warner Robins Daily Sun,* A4.

3. Used by permission.

Chapter Eleven

1. *Shadowlands,* HBO Studios, 1994.

2. Aeschylus, *Agamemnon,* trans. Richmond Lattimore, *Greek Plays in Modern Translation,* ed. Dudley Fitts (New York: The Dial, 1947), 23.

3. C. S. Lewis, *The Problem of Pain* (New York: HarperSanFrancisco, 1996), 91.

4. Sophocles, "Electra," trans. David Greene, *The Complete Greek Tragedies: Sophocles II,* ed. David Greene and Richmond Lattimore (Chicago: University of Chicago Press, 1957), 162.

5. William Wordsworth, "Character of the Happy Warrior," *Wordsworth Complete Poetical Work* (Oxford: Oxford University Press, 1936), 386.

6. Proverbs 17:22.

Chapter Twelve

1. David Edwin Harrell Jr., *Oral Roberts: An American Life* (Bloomington, Ind.: Indiana University Press, 1985), 440, 462.

2. Jean Cocteau, *Diary of an Unknown,* trans. Jesse Browner (New York: Paragon House, 1988), 44.

3. Henry David Thoreau, *The Journal of Henry D. Thoreau,* vol. I-VII (1837–October 1855), ed. Bradford Torrey and Francis H. Allen (New York: Dover, 1962), 152.

4. Os Hillman, "Four Attributes of a Life God Blesses," *Marketplace Meditations,* found at http://www.wowi.net.

5. Edith Schaefer, *L'Abri* (Wheaton, Ill.: Tyndale, 1969), 123.

ABOUT CREATIVE MEMORIES

Creative Memories consultants teach others how to preserve the past, enrich the present, and inspire hope for the future through the creation of keepsake scrapbook photo albums. They provide researched information and one-on-one assistance in Home Classes, Shows, and Workshops.

To locate a consultant near you, contact us at 1-800-341-5275 or visit our Web site at http://www.creativememories.com.

We'd love to hear how making keepsake albums has changed *your* life and the lives of those you love. Send your album-related stories of family, friendship, faith, and more to:

Creative Memories
Attention: Heidi Everett
P.O. Box 1839
St. Cloud, MN 56302-1839

Or visit our Web site at
http://www.creativememories.com
and click on "Share Our Stories."